WHAT IS INTUITION?

Resonance, Connection, and Trusting Intuition on its own Terms

EMILY SADOWSKI, PhD

What is Intuition?
Copyright © 2023 by Emily Sadowski, PhD
www.whatisintuition.ca

All rights reserved. No part of this publication may be reproduced, stored in a retrieval system, or transmitted in any form or by any means, without prior permission in writing from the publisher.

OneCan Press
Ontario, Canada

Paperback ISBN: 978-1-7390002-0-2
E-Book ISBN: 978-1-7390002-1-9

Cover and Text Design:
Kristy Twellmann Hill • umbrellasquared.com
Art Direction: fleck creative

"Whatever is unnamed, undepicted in images, whatever is omitted from biography, censored in collections of letters, whatever is misnamed as something else, made difficult-to-come-by, whatever is buried in the memory by the collapse of meaning under an inadequate or lying language—this will become, not merely unspoken, but unspeakable."[1]
—Adrienne Rich

TABLE OF CONTENTS

    A Note to the Reader viii
1. Speaking the Unspeakable 4
2. What Is Intuition? 26
3. How Does Intuition Work? 56
4. A Praxis for Cultivating Intuition 86
5. Pillar 1: Mindset 94
6. Pillar 2: Awareness 132
7. Pillar 3: Discernment 156
8. Intuition On Its Own Terms 180
    Glossary 190
    Endnotes 196
    Selected Bibliography 202
    Acknowledgements 208
    Author Biography 211

INTRO
A NOTE TO THE READER

WHAT IS INTUITION?

This book is for everyone who wants to better understand what intuition is and why that matters. It's especially for you if you want to feel more connected to your intuition, or crave a more coherent, dynamic relationship between your inner world and outer life. And, it's also for those of us who seek a deeper connection to something *more*.

But this isn't one of those books that simply teaches you how to become more intuitive. There are enough of those how-to intuition books out there. The truth is, you already *are* intuitive, but our minds and internalized values easily get in the way of that.

So rather than how-to, this book is a why-to.

My goal is to start a conversation about something we know is important but is difficult to talk about. Our world is in the midst of a massive paradigm shift. People are becoming more intuitive, and simultaneously are in need of cultivating wise discernment. We're faced with the need to know: What is the right thing to do? What is true? What matters?

And many of us don't trust our intuition. In the privacy of our own minds, many of us are having all kinds of non-ordinary and extra-ordinary awarenesses, but without a context that lets them make sense, we don't always register what they mean, or recognize if they're meaningful at all. Understandably, it can be hard to put intuitive experiences into words, and to put those words into a framework that explains what is even happening.

By the end of the book, you'll be thinking about intuition with a bigger point of view than you're starting with. Most importantly, you will get to know intuition as a relationship you have with yourself; a process of consciousness you can cultivate intentionally.

The ideas in this book began as my PhD research. I use specific vocabulary and concepts that we don't use day-to-day. The glossary is there for a reason. As with any book that addresses some complex ideas, it's more than okay to read slowly, or to let the ideas wash over you. I hope the book becomes something you return to again and again, as a reference. Maybe you'll read with others, in a book group or with friends. In any case, make sure you pick up the readers' discussion guide and other bonus material, available at www.WhatIsIntuition.ca.

Taking up the inner work of developing your intuition is an act of reclamation and resistance to the widespread alienation that exists throughout our culture. By learning to trust our intuitive experiences, we can then show ourselves and others that these experiences are a real and valuable part of human experience. So, thank you for reading. As our world becomes more intuitive, it's also in need of people who are integrating ideas about intuition, resonance, and connection as vital aspects of our everyday experience.

Chapter 1

SPEAKING THE UNSPEAKABLE

Since 2008, I have worked as a scholar of education and transformation, studying and teaching about knowledge and knowledge production, theories of learning, and what it takes to transform how we relate to—and understand—the world. One theme that has always followed me around different teaching and research positions, from London, England, to Vancouver, British Columbia, is contained in the question: *How do people learn to become different from how they are?* In other words, *how do people change?*

These questions are important, beyond the scope of my chosen field of study, Philosophy of Education. We can think about them individually, directing them inward to inform self-development: *How can I become the person I believe I could be? How can I be more of who I am?* For teachers, therapists, coaches, and community and business leaders, these are professional questions that arise every day, with practical and existential implications.

We can also think about these questions collectively. These days, understanding the processes of collective change and transformation seems more important than anything else. If you're paying even a little bit of attention, it's not hard to see that our collective ways have led us towards the brink of literal, existential disaster. Extractive colonial capitalism threatens ecological sustainability—the very sustaining we need to continue living on the planet. Some of us trace the state of our collective as resulting from being disconnected: from a sense of place, a sense of purpose or meaning, or from a relationship to something greater than ourselves. Others are more explicit: climate chaos, inequality, and even many violent conflicts all arise from an approach to understanding the world through the lens of rational analysis.

After years of thinking about personal and collective transformation, I've come to understand that questions of change or transformation can never be separated from the culture, community, or context in which people live and work. In other words, what we believe, what we know, and the range of potential we recognize as being possible (for ourselves individually and collectively) are all shaped by our relationships and our beliefs about the world.

So, what does this have to do with intuition? A lot, it turns out.

Between 2011 and 2017, I found myself studying leadership and transformation in a faculty of education, in a program that looked at teaching and learning through the lenses of culture, consciousness, and ecology. There, researching questions about the aims of education—what we teach and, more importantly, *what we don't teach*—I became increasingly interested in what gets left out of the curriculum, either on purpose or by 'sins of omission.' This is where my interest in intuition development was sparked. I would regularly encounter the idea that intuition is a key characteristic of mindful, skillful leaders. Intuition would show up in my research about how to best teach in support of developing students' leadership, agency, and self-awareness. Intuition was clearly an important ingredient in teaching, learning, and simply living a good life, yet it occurred to me that I had never once encountered the concept of intuition throughout all my years of schooling.

Growing up, the word 'intuition' was not in my vocabulary nor anywhere in my sphere of awareness. I didn't hear the word at school, and I never heard the concept in my family home. No one ever spoke to me about the ability to hear my inner voice or to 'just know' or about relying on inner wisdom to make decisions or to make sense of situations. I definitely wasn't aware of the possibility for *psychic* intuitive experience. If anything, I was probably surrounded by people who ignored their intuitive feelings to make way for being 'acceptable' or 'rational.'

I mean, I must have known that intuition exists. I had heard about gut feelings and knew that they are supposed to be trusted. But I'm not sure I ever had one. As a young adult, I had read about intuitive and psychic experiences in New Age books like *The Celestine Prophecy*. I remember borrowing a roommate's book by New Age self-help author Sonia Choquette that taught people to recognize and trust their 'vibes.' That book was filled with anecdotes and written by a great storyteller—and I devoured it in an afternoon. I loved the idea that people could be more intuitive, even if I didn't catch on that it could apply to me.

That whole time, I didn't think I knew much about intuition, but in retrospect, I was having intuitive experiences all the time—just without the vocabulary to know that's what it was. My close friend and I shared a connection we called 'the hippie phone.' Sometimes we would inadvertently call each other at the very same moment. Other times, one of us would be thinking of the other and then get a call or text soon after. I now know that experiences like this are fairly common. Even accounting for confirmation bias, many people report telephone telepathy as a feature of their close connections.[i] For me, experiencing the hippie phone was a clue that I was connected to a field of awareness that teachers like Choquette and others spoke about, even when I didn't have a concrete way of integrating what they pointed to.

---

i   IONS is currently running a study about telephone telepathy. See more about IONS and their research at https://noetic.org/

While it might sound strange coming from someone who has studied and written about intuition for over a decade, I never thought of myself as particularly intuitive. My intuitive capacity ebbs and flows. I'm intuitive in some ways, less so in others. For instance, I'm pretty consistent in being able to see the big picture and in perceiving connections between things, but the aha moments and sudden, certain awarenesses are less frequent in my experience. The truth is, my intuitive function continues to evolve.

For many years, intuition would show up for me in the form of library angels[ii]—that's what I called my knack for coming across just the right title on a bookshelf that would get me to the next place in my research. I have played with this ability sometimes, wandering through the stacks at a library or a bookstore until feeling drawn to a certain title or series. Other times, I've had strong, intuitive hits about my personal safety, like the feeling I should take a different route home from my usual one. I always try to follow these inclinations and assume that they are helping me avoid harm. But of course, there's no way to confirm that they are real, since we can only know what actually happens—not what might have.

Now that I teach and coach others to feel more connected to their intuition, something I hear from clients a lot is that they know their intuition in retrospect. They realize later that they "just knew" but at the time didn't make the connection.

---

ii Library angels are the name I use for my experience of bibliomancy, a divination practice that involves using intuition as a guide for choosing and opening a selection from a book and using those lines as oracular information. I use the word 'angels' kind of tongue-in-cheek; I don't believe there are actual angels guiding my way (though if you do, that's great) but rather an **intra-active** intuitive relationship at work, allowing me to be sensitive to information in that way.

Often, those experiences don't register because, like me, people don't realize they're intuitive. But when we dig in and create a personal history of intuitive experiences, it turns out there have been moments throughout most people's lives where their intuition showed up—they just maybe didn't recognize it as such.

Okay, do me a favour. Take a minute to think back across your life. Do you have any personal anecdotes about intuition? When did you—or someone you know—have an uncanny intuitive hit? I'm pretty confident that, whether you listened at the time or not, you'll have at least a couple stories about intuition in your pocket.

When I really started studying intuition and psychic development, my own intuitive hits started coming in faster, more often, and more clearly. I remember one day in the Fall of 2011. I had just been to the library and was sitting among my haul of books: books about cultivating creativity, about the energetic centre at the heart, about how and why intuition is valuable to teachers, business leaders, and creatives. Sitting among my books and notebooks, I suddenly thought about some other books I had recently ordered online. I wondered to myself, "When were those supposed to be delivered again?" Not a minute later, the doorbell rang upstairs. The books were being delivered! Cool, right!?

A similar thing happened with telephone telepathy. I started getting really good at guessing who that text was from before looking at the phone. And more and more often, I'd think of someone and moments later get a call from them. All of this 'just knowing' was uncanny; I had no way to explain what was happening within my limited way of making sense of the world. I realized I needed to try to understand these intuitive experiences through a more expansive lens.

Intuition became a more conscious, personal factor for me when I first learned to practice *reiki*, an energy healing modality with roots in Japan. The induction ritual to reiki is a series of attunements[iii] that connects individuals to the reiki energy, and I received my first attunement in July 2005. Immediately after that induction, I noticed a small-but-insistent awareness that let me know things in an intuitive way.

The very next day, as usual, I went to work at my sales job in a store. I remember taking a call from a customer who wanted to give her order over the phone. We went through the regular procedure; I took her phone number, and we confirmed the product code. But as I was hanging up, I suddenly knew that something was going to get messed up with this order. There was nothing specific that led me to know this, just an insistent, general awareness that I would need to follow up on something. Sure enough, it turned out the item she had ordered was no longer available.

Later that same day, while occupied with something else in the showroom, I heard the phone ring in the background of my awareness. (Again, with the phone!) Instantly, I thought, "Oh that's my dad calling." And I was right. There was really no reason for me to think that. The store's phone rang hundreds of times a day, and my dad rarely called me at work. But there it was, the subtle-but-certain awareness, almost heard as a voice in my mind, letting me know things I had no reason to know.

[iii] Reiki attunements are a series of gestures performed by the teacher on the aura of the student. The effect of the attunement is to transfer or transmit the specific vibration of reiki energy to the student, for them to experience it directly.

These are small, and maybe even insignificant, examples of intuitive experiences. But the information I intuited that day is less important than the fact that I had access to it in the first place. I now understand that the reiki attunement had connected me to my intuitive sense by enhancing my awareness of energy itself. Beyond the information I was accessing, what's significant is that I was having the experience—from within—of sudden, certain, *accurate*, intuitive knowing. I had become more connected with the energetic fields around me, or maybe it's more accurate to say I became more sensitive to being connected with the consciousness of the universe at large. And it was paying off in intuitive experience.

Now, this is not a book about reiki, and I'm not saying that reiki is what you need to be more in touch with your intuition. I won't be suggesting that learning any one modality is The Way to cultivate intuitive awareness. But usually, we do need something to remind us of the connection we can have with the energy of the universe.

Reiki worked for me like a fast road to developing my intuition. I had been disconnected from this sensitivity within myself. Truly, most people living in the overdeveloped, Global North are disconnected from the subtle realms of experience. We simply don't have space for psychic experience in our frames of reference. I needed a boost of resonance, and a reiki attunement provided it for me.

Some of you will have an intuitive connection that is more resilient; that doesn't wane, despite cultural practices that try to eliminate our awareness of it, even withstanding a whole education system that requires us to ignore energy, tells us spooky stories about it, and encourages us to look for answers anywhere but within. Maybe you have been able to resist this inculcation into the rational-analytic mode. But even if you consider yourself intuitive, it's often kept separate. Like a Clark Kent/Superman situation, our intuition is something we do privately, without anyone else knowing, and we don't credit it.

For me, learning reiki let me experience my intuition in a new way. Reiki helped me experience my intuition by opening up a range of neglected perceptive possibility, based in a deepened relationship between myself and my surroundings.

My supercharged intuitive ability didn't last, by the way. I didn't suddenly become psychic like a character in a movie would have; and after a while, those experiences happened less often. It was only after some time *practicing* reiki, developing a regular meditation practice, and cultivating the inner energetic body that I have developed a sustained sensitivity to that resonance of vibes. I'd later learn that this inner work is known to support intuitive development—and that almost any meditative, inner-directed mind-body practice supports intuition, which makes sense, knowing what I now do about what intuition is and how it works.

My intuitive capacity showed up because the attunement ritual (and anchoring it through practice) had ignited an awareness in me, of the energetic resonance between myself (the knower) and knowledge (the known). I was able to perceive information as if it came from within, experiencing a continuity between myself and not-myself, between experience and information, between immediacy and distance. By experiencing the vibrational patterns of energy through my body, I perceived information moving as energy, flowing throughout matter, even crossing the boundaries of time and space.

Clearly, there was a connection between intuition and the role of energy, consciousness, and context that my upbringing and education had neglected to let me know about.

In retrospect, I see that studying intuition was a roundabout way to understand and unpack this very connection, which reflects a paradigmatic shift I see happening in the world more broadly—one that's bringing forward the role of unseen energy, interconnectedness, and relatedness in how we construct our framing of the world around us.

This emergent paradigm includes **spirituality**[iv] as a matter of course; an acceptance (or at least an agnostic willingness to consider the possibility) that *something* exists beyond the human plane of experience. Some refer to this shift in orientation as a new age, and I'm okay with that designation—though I am critical of the ways New Age secular spirituality has been appropriative of many of the world's traditions. I know that many people feel an aversion to spirituality, but I readily admit that some of what I'm talking about here is **woo**—I don't consider that an insult. I understand spirituality as a way to pursue meaning and purpose, and an acknowledgment of the holistic, multidimensional connections that run between all things in our world.

But no surprise, I encountered a lot of resistance trying to bring an explanation of this awareness into the academy.

As an educator, I'm all too aware that, in addition to teaching information and knowledge, education is a process that teaches people how to *be* in the world. To me, this is the most important role for education. But like many others, I'm not satisfied with educating people how to best be in the world that currently exists.

---

iv   Words in bold are defined in the Glossary.

I'm thinking ahead and interested in how to educate for the kind of society we want to have—rather than the one we currently live in. My research has been guided by curiosity about the role of education in this uncertain state of becoming and how it can act as a process of cultivating the kind of humans we want to live in community with: those who are leaders in their own contexts and those who act with agency and integrity in their own lives.

Over the years, I have seen changes in our culture that signal a new and evolving interest—away from a version of success that emphasizes capital accumulation of material things and towards a version of success that involves personal happiness and psychological ease. In this shift, taking place in the context of a culture that is organized to limit peace, joy, and creativity, I recognize an orientation towards meaning and fulfillment. People are waking up and asking themselves, "What matters?"

I am thrilled to see these habits and understandings becoming more widely shared, more widely recognized as important elements of a life well lived. My research led me to think deeply about how to educate in a way that supports the paradigmatic shift underway: how we can be more receptive to recognizing a participatory, creative nature of reality; collectively move away from a shared belief that the world is ultimately knowable (and therefore conquerable); and be more invested in the process—rather than the product—of lived experience. Intuition became an emblem of that shift, because we can't understand intuition on its own terms while ignoring the **transpersonal** dimensions of unseen energy and consciousness.

So, while this is a book about intuition—what it is and why that matters—it's also about the **metaphysics** that frame intuition as making sense, and the ideas and practices that can help us navigate towards an improved relationship with our own intuitive sense.

Let's be honest. It's hard to talk about the experience of intuiting. What does intuition feel like!? How do we know if the tingle in our belly is intuition or something else (like indigestion!)? Clients describe funny feelings, just knowing something, or other experiences they can't put into words. Intuition is hard to talk about because it mostly takes place below the threshold of awareness, in a part of ourselves that doesn't lend itself to words. The same part where feelings, dreams, and insight reside.

This whole problem is made worse by the fact that, collectively, we haven't talked to each other much about intuition. We say "intuition" and leave it at that, assuming we're all talking about the same thing. (Spoiler alert: We're not.) Intuition can refer to spiritual insight, to the spark of genius that tells us how to solve a tricky problem, and to the capacity for sensing the vibe in a room full of people, among other things. What do all these experiences even have in common?

Plus, living as we do in a culture wedded to knowing things *objectively*, the subjective nature of intuition makes it nearly impossible to share the experience with each other. We might know what intuition is, intuitively. But when it comes to having a shared vocabulary for talking with each other about intuition, it's just not there.

It's also hard to talk about intuition in terms of the **worldview** or framework that lets intuition make sense. I'm not just trying to give us vocabulary for talking about what intuition is; I'm trying to show that many intuitive experiences are made possible by our situatedness in a unified, multidimensional field of quantum consciousness. Thinking and writing about intuition has been, for me, a way of pointing to this transpersonal consciousness, and I'm excited and inspired by how this understanding might help us know ourselves as connected to something greater—and as powerful knowers.

You might want to know more about what intuition is because you know it's a valuable resource, something you can look to and rely on to make good decisions; that can help you know what's best or right. You might already have a connection to your intuition and want to know what it's all about.

Maybe you're already inclined to trust that intuition is a reasonable and realistic way to access knowing. But you might not be fully convinced just yet. The idea of psychic intuition might feel especially challenging or confusing.

If you're like many people I know, you might value intuition in general but don't always trust that it delivers quality information. You might talk yourself out of what you know intuitively. You might overthink or doubt your way into confusion rather than trust your intuitive experiences.

Or you might be someone who guides others to trust their intuition. You might be searching for a framework and vocabulary for encouraging your clients or students to cultivate their own intuitive function.

It's not easy to talk about this stuff, but the effort is worth it because the concepts that help us speak about intuitive experiences also help us understand, accept, and then cultivate those experiences. And they help us understand and accept who and what we are.

I decided to write this book because it was a book I could have really used back when I was a student of philosophy of education, eager to dive into the subject of intuition and leadership from a trustworthy, 'scholarly' source that also acknowledged the transpersonal element of intuitive experience. At the time, I was trying to understand what intuition is because I knew that developing intuition was an important aspect of leadership and transformation. And like the good scholar I was, I wanted backup.

But when I went to the university library, almost all the references to intuition I found corresponded to a version of intuition I couldn't relate to. My library angels were coming up empty!

Everywhere I looked, whether in education theory, psychology, **epistemology** (the study of knowledge), or leadership studies, the word 'intuition' meant something other than the psychic foreknowledge, telepathy, and gut feelings I had encountered in my own life experience and that were described in the New Age books I had read.

Instead, some of the texts and references revealed a bias *against* intuition. Writers used the word intuition to mean a guess, ill-informed assumption, or expectation—something we get fooled by. They contrasted intuition with so-called better ways to know: reason, intellect, and rationality. I would come across sentences like, "Contrary to the intuition, my reasoning shows...," making intuition into a counterpoint.

There's an optical illusion sometimes used to make this point. It's the one that shows two horizontal lines, one above the other, with arrows on their ends, and they look like they're different lengths. Your intuition (here meaning 'unthinking first impression') is that one line is longer than the other—but that's an illusion. If you take the time to measure both lines, you see that they are the same length. In this example, popular in philosophy textbooks, 'intuition' is synonymous with wrong or misguided, used as a setup to make way for more reasonable, analytic arguments.

Many of the references I found positioned intuition as an exclusively cognitive ability; a kind of fast thinking that happens as a result of subconscious recall.[v] The concept here is that a person can accrue a depth of experience in some area and then make fast, confident judgments or assessments without thinking about them. More accurately, the thinking takes place subconsciously, without the person's awareness, so that it only *seems* like intuitive content arising spontaneously, out of nowhere. (But it really comes from a storage of knowledge built over time and experience.)

Intuition-as-expertise is a particularly popular explanation for intuition, and while it is a reasonable way to explain a lot of intuitive experience, it's incomplete. Personally, I have absolutely known things intuitively that could not have arisen out of a subconscious storage chamber. That phone call from my dad wasn't something I knew from acquired expertise. It was a sudden, certain awareness that really did come from nowhere (at least, nowhere I could point to and no storehouse of experience that would lead me to knowing this mundane, unimportant information—no offense, Dad). Yet many of the theorists I encountered who advocated for intuition's value in teaching, learning, leading, and innovation were loyal to this incomplete, cognition-friendly definition of intuition.

More often than not, I found that scholars were meticulously careful to distance themselves from any association with intuition as woo-woo, mystical, or extra-sensory. Some even added a kind

---

v   Many people think about intuition like Malcolm Gladwell's concept of *Blink*—fast thinking. Even though Gladwell himself denied that the concept was intuition, it gets taken up that way.

of disclaimer. They wanted to make clear that what *they* meant by intuition was a completely rational, logical, normal experience, and that whatever the New Agers meant by intuition—psychic experiences like telepathic communication and pre-cognitive awareness—was something different from these highly respectable leadership instincts they were promoting.

I was so disappointed by these disclaimers. I still am, whenever I see thought leaders trying to establish respectability at the expense of peoples' lived experiences. The advocate in me stepped up and became worried that future students interested in the concept and potential for intuition might be convinced by these authority figures that psychic experiences aren't real—they can't be real, they're pseudo-science—and be dissuaded from bringing intuition into their classrooms or helping their clients be more intuitive. The idea that, in the 21st century, there are still 'experts' working to dismiss people's connection to intuitive experience lit a fire under me.

And yet, I get it. These were serious scholars with a lot to lose if people thought they were aligning with the para-psychological interest in intuition that has since, by the way, become even more popular.

A famous philosopher once confirmed this for me straight out. After publishing a book about intuition and education that hinted at the relevance of psychic phenomena, she purposefully toned down the way she spoke about it because her curiosity about psychic experience attracted too many "out-there" characters—not the scholars and educators she was trying to appeal to.

As I came to understand, these theorists were not only defending their reputations—they were defending their worldviews. If they allowed psychic intuition into their framework, they would be opening up the possibility that consciousness can transcend space and time, or that the mind and body are integrally connected in ways that our science doesn't currently recognize. This would be a devastating disruption for anyone invested in a materialist, rational view of the world (which most educated, intelligent people are). Without an acceptable theory of intuition that makes sense to who and what we think we are, it's much easier to simply ignore, dismiss, or deny the existence of psychic intuition. We put it away in a corner of the mind and don't think about it.

Among psychologists, philosophers, spiritual teachers, leadership coaches, and other professionals, there is a lot at stake for explaining intuition. Different camps set up their own ways of conceptualizing and defining what intuition is, where it comes from, and what its capabilities are. Each definition can reveal what a person believes about consciousness and about the nature of reality (metaphysics). In other words, what we think intuition *is* depends on what we believe about the world more broadly—what we believe about consciousness, energy, knowledge, and what we *are*.

For example, if you believe that consciousness is entirely an epi-phenomenon of the brain's neuro-chemical processes, then you will want intuition to be defined as something material, like a result of expertise and experience that arises to conscious awareness as needed. Or as subconscious cognition, where the brain figures something out based on barely perceptible clues, and processes this data below the threshold of consciousness.

Alternatively, if you believe that individual consciousness is connected to a universally available collective consciousness, you might interpret intuition as direct connection between yourself and the multidimensional universe. Or if you're more inclined towards religious iconography, you might conceptualize intuition as communication from guides or a team of angels that has your best interests at heart. None of these interpretations are wrong per se; they are just specific and diverse ways to understand what is happening, based in differing worldviews. Most significantly, the underlying beliefs are relevant because what we believe about intuition helps shape how we experience it.

In any case, we shouldn't let ignorance about what intuition is interfere with learning to cultivate it. In order to awaken our intuitive capacity, we need to be able to speak about intuition. Even if the language is clunky, even if the words aren't exactly right. As the poet Adrienne Rich wrote, "Whatever is unnamed, undepicted in images, whatever is omitted from biography, censored in collections of letters, whatever is misnamed as something else, made difficult-to-come-by, whatever is buried in the memory by the collapse of meaning under an inadequate or lying language—this will become, not merely unspoken, but unspeakable."

Intuition has become one of those unspeakable things, and this book gives us language that will help to un-bury our experiences. The more we speak about our intuitive experience, the more we'll be *able* to speak about it.

INTUITION ON ITS OWN TERMS

My studies in philosophy and critical theory helped me learn that if a framework (or set of beliefs) is too limited to account for lived experiences, that's a problem with the framework—not the experience. So, my research into resonance, connection, and intuitive experience began with the concept of intuition as it appears in the frameworks of new age self-help books that teach about intuition. These books showed me what it looks like to validate intuitive experiences like energy sensitivity, vibes, and so-called extra-sensory perception, while being unapologetic about the secular spirituality that inform their view on what intuition is.

I looked at these explanations for intuition in light of some of the many critical theories of knowledge that show us how knowledge and its production is a political process. I explored feminist theories of knowledge that are rooted in the knower's concrete and practical lived experience. I looked to contemplative educators and their theories of knowledge that assume "the kind of knowledge content we have is vitally dependent on the shape of the container—that is, the knowing person."[2] And I turned to Indigenous theories of knowledge that teach how knowledge comes "from Being, an intimate visceral and psychic relationship with specific places, spaces, sounds and faces on Earth (and beyond)."[3]

The thing is, knowledge is not neutral. We're all always perceiving the world through our worldview, our lens, and our assumptions about what is good and what is true. What gets thought of as reasonable and even real are conditioned by our cultural values and practices. The process of becoming educated is an initiation into a particular framework of knowledge (an epistemological framework). And the framework that is currently in fashion is one that is alienated from direct experience. Instead of immersing people in the world where they are and allowing their inner and outer context to become known, what gets taught and learned are de-contextualized knowledge practices.

Through my studies, and with a commitment to understanding intuition on its own terms, I learned that intuition needs a connected worldview to make sense. Intuition is a process. Or a system. It is complex, relational, and inter-subjective. Understanding intuition requires a framework that's totally different from the mainstream, colonized, alienated, de-contextualized approach to knowledge where things are seen as static (dead!).

Intuition is really misunderstood because there's been a very deep taboo against aspects of consciousness that don't conform to the prevailing framework. It feels risky to 'admit' to intuitive experience. And I want to do a good job of putting into words what is so hard to put into words: the most personal and subjective experiences of feeling connected, supported, and belonging to our own lives and to life in general. These are spiritual matters and they deserve to be recognized as such.

As I write these words, I'm all too aware of how risky it feels to write about spirituality so explicitly. The rational-intellectual-analytical mode that dominates our culture does not have much time for spirituality and the unseen world. And I'm imagining you reading this, possibly having some sticky feelings of your own about the idea of metaphysics and spirituality. The risk I'm taking in writing about intuition as spiritual feels similar to the risk each of us faces when trusting our intuition: being asked to trust what can't be seen or even clearly conceptualized, within an intellectual climate that tells us—through the internalized Voice of Reason—that our intuitive experiences *can't* be real, since they don't conform to the standards of knowledge we have been taught are true.

Languaging our experience lets us see patterns, connections, and systems.[4] By talking about intuition, we can recognize it as a common, normal part of human conscious awareness—rather than as being incoherent, exceptional, or extra-ordinary. Learning how to speak about intuitive experience becomes a way to validate and authorize intuitive experiences, the intuitive mode itself, and the realities of consciousness that make intuition possible.

The worldview that lets intuition make sense has been out of fashion for too long.

The hegemony of analysis and rationality has led to an unfortunate situation where a lot of people simply don't recognize (or admit to) intuitive experience. And that means we learn not to trust our inner knowing, our inner awareness, our inner-directed connection—whatever you want to call it (if we register it at all). So my goal with this book is to bridge the gap in understanding and support a collective shift, one that's now recognizing, "Hey. It *is* important to talk about intuition." One that's empowering us to know—and validate—our lived experiences of *just knowing*.

Here's where this book is headed: First, we'll take a deep dive into what intuition is; its characteristics and nuances. By the end of chapter 2 you'll be equipped with a vocabulary to describe the wide range of intuitive experiences and how they can show up.

Then, I'm going to present a 'logic' that lets intuition make sense on its own terms—a holistic, both/and logic that embraces uncertainty and nonduality and relies on the person having the experience to assess its truth. As you read chapter 3, I encourage you to drop the need to understand intuition according to analytic logic and rational proof and instead to accept uncertainty and paradox as a feature of intuitive experience.

And of course, I'm going to talk about how we can cultivate intuition. Chapters 4-7 explore three core pillars of intuition development that you'll find in many intuition development programs. By practicing self-awareness and learning about ourselves and our potentials, cultivating intuition engages us in a kind of inner work that has been done since antiquity as a form of education aimed at becoming better leaders and better people in general.

As we undertake the process of developing intuition, we are contributing to an emergent paradigm; one where we recognize our interconnectedness and the nature of nondual consciousness, and that what we do has an effect in and on the world.

Throughout all of this, please remember: Our judgment is skewed by what we think reality entails. Disconnection, **alienation**, mechanism, binary and dualistic hierarchies are so embedded in our belief structures that they shape what we experience of the world around us—and how we experience it.

And still, we are intuitive.

Chapter 2
WHAT IS INTUITION?

As far as words go, 'intuition' is a vocabulary workhorse. We use that one word to explain such a wide spectrum of inner-directed experiences of perception and awareness. From its Latin origins—*in tueri* (to look at or towards; to contemplate) or *intuitus* (the act of achieving knowledge from direct perception or contemplation)—we can understand the modern word *intuition* to mean an internal perception or inner awareness, where knowledge, awareness, insight, or understanding arrives—*or feels like it arrives*—from within.

A common contemporary definition for intuition is *knowing without being able to trace how we know*, a phrase that covers a whole range of inner knowing, including things we know but never learned, things we can sense without involving any of the ordinary senses, things that seem impossible to know (such as telepathic awareness—knowing what's in someone else's mind), gut feelings, precognition, 'just knowing,' knowing from and through the heart, knowing by becoming one with the essence of a thing, aha moments, insight, knowing when something is right or wrong for you. And the list goes on.

All of these 'versions' of intuition fall into one of three categories of experience: implicit knowledge, energetic sensitivity, or psychic intuition[i]. These categories are convenient, but they shouldn't be taken as strictly distinct. It's much more likely that intuition draws on any or all of these categories—possibly at the same time.

IMPLICIT KNOWLEDGE: Sometimes the word 'intuition' stands in when we can't otherwise identify how we know a thing. One version of this intuitive experience, fast thinking, is the go-to

---

[i] These categories come from the research organization HeartMath, www.heartmath.com/.

definition for many theorists, probably because it centres the role of the mind. This is implicit knowledge, or deep expertise, the kind of knowing that usually happens when knowledge acquired in the past (either consciously or subconsciously) comes forward suddenly, often in a circumstance where new understanding is required. In design and development, we say a product or service is 'intuitive' when a user's experience is easy and accessible to non-experts. This category also covers aha moments, intuitive problem solving, and many other instances of *knowing without knowing how we know*.

There's a strong connection between intuition and other implicit, inner-directed experiences, like instinct, imagination, insight, and inspiration, so trying to distinguish where these end and intuition begins gets fuzzy. But when we use the word as a catch-all for every time there's no thinking involved, intuition too easily gets lumped in with guesses and assumptions. Like when 'intuitive' is used as an excuse, a way to justify unconscious bias or other unjustified belief.

ENERGETIC SENSITIVITY: This category refers to the subtle ability of the nervous system to perceive and respond to energetic shifts, whether they come from within, from other people, from collective moods, or even earth changes. (Like when people—and many animals—can intuitively register earthquakes before they happen.) In this category, we can include bodily signals that pick up vibes, the sense of being stared at, and ways of knowing characteristic to parts of the **psyche** that don't use words, like the imagination and dream-states.

The energy we're talking about here is unseen, but that doesn't mean it's not real! On the contrary, because it's real in the non-cognitive, non-verbal sense, these kinds of intuitive experiences can sometimes feel *more* real than concepts or thoughts. They occur to us directly, without filtering through thoughts or words. But a risk with these energetic intuitive experiences is that, because they occur in subtle, subjective registers, they can sometimes be easy to miss or dismiss.

Empathic intuition is a version of energetic sensitivity. It's when we know something through resonance, almost becoming one with the content. Intuitive movement teacher Wendy Palmer describes her connection with horses this way, as an empathic shared knowledge that allows them to communicate without words. This kind of intuitive awareness shows up in therapeutic contexts with human clients, too, when counsellors or coaches get an intuitive hit about how their client is feeling or what they need.

TRANSPERSONAL (OR PSYCHIC) INTUITION: The third category of intuitive experience is the ability to know or sense something across distances of space or time. What we're talking about here is 'extra-sensory perception' (ESP), sometimes referred to as *non-local intuition* or *psi*, when the speaker wants to be clear that they don't think of this ability as 'extra' but rather within the intrinsic range of human sensory capacity. Also sometimes called 'para-psychological,' these intuitive experiences can't be explained by fast thinking, unconscious processing, or even energetic sensitivity.

Psychic comes from the Greek word *psyche*, meaning soul or spirit. Psyche is typically translated as 'mind' (as in psychology: the study of mind), but I prefer the way the philosopher-psychologist C.G. Jung understands psyche: the totality of conscious and unconscious processes we experience, including individual and collective aspects.[5] Using this definition, we can frame psychic intuition as a mode of communication or interaction between the conscious and unconscious mind. Psychic intuition gets experienced many different ways, including through dreams, pre-cognitive awareness, prescience (foreknowledge), clairvoyance (clear seeing), clairaudience (clear hearing), clairsentience (clear feeling), claircognizance (just knowing), and telepathy.

INTUITION, INSIGHT, AND INSTINCT

Intuition is often called on to make good decisions, both in the immediate and ordinary contexts of our daily lives, as well as in the larger sense of the direction of our soul's development. The tradition of this connection goes back at least as far as Socrates and his relationship to his daemon, or inner teacher/inner guide, at the foundation of Western philosophy.

A contemporary version of the archetype of the daemon role is the intuitive ally, an aspect of the **self** that acts as a wise guide or inner GPS. Clarissa Pinkola Estés links intuition to an inherited ability to perceive what is right, writing that intuition acts "like a wise old woman who is with you always, who tells you exactly what the matter is, tells you exactly whether you need to go left or right."[6] Estés tells the story of Vasalisa, whose dying mother gives her a doll. This doll, she is told, will be with her always; she only needs to be fed. Vasalisa carries the doll everywhere—in her pocket—to consult as needed, as her intuitive guide. Like Vasalisa's doll, if we feed and care for our intuitive nature, she'll never steer us wrong. By cultivating that relationship, intuition becomes like a decision-making guide we can totally trust, as long as we listen. She just needs to be nurtured.

As an ally, intuition is tied to the innate sense of knowing we call *instinct*; knowledge built into our DNA and inherited over millennia. The instinctive impulse to survive and thrive is an ancient aspect of human consciousness, comprising our animal abilities and awarenesses that helped ensure our species' survival. Intuition may be a distilled, evolved form of instinct, a development of the pre-verbal, nascent intelligence that contributed to the direction of human development.

Jung pointed out this connection when he described intuition as "instinctive apprehension," a phrase I love because it evokes embodied experiences like gut feelings, 'spidey-sense,' and other relational intuitive experiences such as telephone telepathy, mother's intuition, and the sense of being stared at[ii] (when you 'just know' you're being watched, even if you don't see the watcher.) Many of us have had—or at least know others who have had—intuitive experiences that could be connected to instinct, such as sensing police radar around the next corner, knowing when a friend is about to call, or the uncanny awareness of feeling, from a distance, the moment a loved one has passed away. We could also include here neuro-biological experiences like electromagnetic sensitivity that allow us to anticipate and sense things in our environment, even if they're just out of reach of the ordinary senses.

It seems that 'instinctive apprehension' might be something we need to be safe, well, and connected in a holistic sense, especially to the extent that we can learn to discern intuition from fear, anxiety, and projection. There are so many examples of uncanny senses that seem to arise from the instinct of knowing when danger is imminent, even when there are no external signals: nothing to see, smell, hear, or touch, yet something in us *knows*. One psychic

---

[ii] I first heard this phrase from Rupert Sheldrake, in his book of the same name.

who can anticipate earthquakes around the world, not just where she lives, describes this ability in herself as a "human tuning fork."[iii]

But intuition is subtly different from instinct in two important ways. One, it lets us know things that don't necessarily connect to our safety and survival. We often intuit things that are quite trivial, and experience intuition in areas of our lives that would not have been encountered by our ancestors.

And two, when Jung or Estés frame our intuition as being like an instinctual ally, it's understood that making use of that allyship requires a well-articulated relationship to our inner nature—the kind of relationship cultivated through contemplative and other self-development practices. Instinct alone doesn't seem to require self-awareness in the way intuition seems to.

It's useful to consider the instinctual lineage of our intuitive abilities because it shows us the range of what intuition is good for. Humans come equipped with the will to survive, thrive, and create. Intentionally engaging with the instinct for well-being might help us make better choices to support long-term, collective thriving.

But the connection between instinct and intuition also points to an anxiety about individual and collective well-being: If our instincts are suppressed or damaged to the extent that we can't make skillful use of this function, that suggests we need to proactively minimize and correct the damage we do to instinct through acculturation and education.

---

iii See https://www.starcana.com/

Knowing about these categories of intuitive experience can help us parse out what intuition is. But still, when we're trying to have conversations about intuition, it might be a problem that 'intuition' means too many things to different people.

Sometimes people say 'intuition' and mean the *outcome* or *content* of inner experience. Here, they're referring to some knowledge, awareness, discovery, insight, or understanding gained as a result of intuiting. They might say, "I had an intuition." Or "I had a feeling" or "I had a hunch." This content can be as mundane as finding your lost keys or as transcendent as recognizing the absolute unity of all conscious awareness. (Big range, right?)

So here we have *an* intuition, the product of intuition. Are you still with me? This use of the word is tricky because it can make us expect a neatly contained packet of insight or information. Something we can distinguish from other thoughts or feelings or knowings. It implies that intuitive content should be specific and clear, which you've probably figured out by now it often isn't.

But over here we have intuition as the *source* of intuitive content. You'll hear people say, "My intuition told me that…" This use is tricky, too, because it assigns *agency* to the intuitive sense as a source, cause, or originating mechanism of intuitive experience. Depending on your beliefs, you might understand this source as a guide, your higher self, the subconscious mind, collective awareness, or something else. (Please use whatever word or phrase or idea resonates with you here. My goal throughout the book is to offer options so you can recognize your own experience, while minimizing the things you need to believe in to have a good relationship with your intuition.) This usage implies that 'intuition' is like an external or separate entity; again, something we can point to, concrete or objective.

Within the linguistic structure of English, both these common uses of the word 'intuition' imply that intuition is a bounded, specific thing. It's concrete—it starts and ends. We can point to it and should be able to definitively say, "This is intuition" or "That isn't intuition." Through language, we can lead ourselves to believe that we should be able to distinguish intuition from any other inner awareness. And that if we're not able to simply intuit and know definitively what we have experienced—then we're not intuitive.

As an alternative, I propose we refer to intuitive *experience*: a function, process, or mode of consciousness. This way of referring to intuition centres the intuiting person—the person having the experience—and the relationship they have to their own consciousness. This use, like so much of what we think and understand about intuition, comes from Jung.

Jung taught that intuition is a psychological "type,"[iv] his language for mode or function of consciousness. Another way of saying this is that intuition is a way (or style) of knowing, rather than a skill or ability. Jung's type framework recognizes intuition as a kind of aptitude, one of four innate modes of consciousness we are most likely to rely on in a variety of configurations. In that framework, intuition is paired with sensation as the two "irrational" functions that perceive and receive content. The other two types, feeling and thinking, are the rational functions, which means they are secondary, in that they make sense of the initial input provided by intuition and sensation.

Like all the psychological types, intuition can be either introverted or extroverted, referring to the direction of input. In the

---

iv You might know about this categorizing from the Myers-Briggs Type Indicator, which is based on Jung's work.

extroverted direction, the content is external, coming from out in the world. Here, intuition is like a nose that sniffs out what's possible. It recognizes potential and orients us to perceive what may be upcoming, impending, or just beyond the horizon. Introverted intuition is more difficult to put into words; it receives input from within. Said another way, it perceives the contents of our own consciousness. In this introverted direction, intuition acts as the inner voice and gives rise to experiences like sudden understandings and aha moments.

When I say "intuition," I am usually referring to the intuitive mode of consciousness. Like Jung, I'm referring to intuition as an experience: a way of knowing, a mode of consciousness, or style of processing. Sometimes I'll also refer to an 'intuitive way of being,' meaning an approach to navigating through the world that seems to flow naturally, rather than being stultified by doubt, analysis, or over-thinking.

WHY DOES IT MATTER?

The diverse usage of the concept of intuition means it's very likely we're not all talking about the same thing when we say 'intuition.' But looking at this range of intuitive experiences as a whole, it's clear there are similarities, no matter what version of intuition we're talking about. What makes these diverse experiences intuition? How is putting together clues from our environment (i.e., implicit knowledge) the same function as tapping into a universal consciousness that transcends space and time? It's a really good question, and we'll get there! But for now, it's important to know that our beliefs about consciousness, reality, and the ways of the world help structure what we understand intuition to be.

A lack of clarity about what intuition *is* isn't always a problem, per se. But if you work with others to support their intuition or if you want to get better acquainted with your own intuitive capacity, it's a good idea to know what you mean. As an inner, subjective experience, intuition is already hard enough to talk about. And a cultural taboo around consciousness has left us without much shared language to speak about intuitive experience. There's so much embedded shaming and authority-claiming around intuition!

It becomes a problem when someone tries to claim, "Oh, this range of experiences is intuitive, and that other range is…bunk." Throughout my time in academia, I found that people would rather wriggle themselves into a corner than admit that intuitive experience is diverse and includes aspects of consciousness that get categorized as 'paranormal' and 'extra-ordinary' … if it meant they could stay 'respectable.' I met plenty of 'experts' and scholars who absolutely denied the reality of psychic experience and insisted that intuition was a function of expertise.

Intuition-as-expertise sits more comfortably in a mind-oriented, rational-materialist framework. And if you're wedded to that framework, all intuitive experience has to be understood as a subconscious process of fast thinking, happening the way you'd expect: a rational process taking place just beneath the surface of conscious awareness. Of course, this framing misses the point. Overlooking the role of energy, resonance, and the nonlocality of information, it necessarily excludes aspects of intuition that can't be accounted for this way, including nonlocal, empathic, and precognitive intuitive experiences.

You can start to see why so many of us don't recognize our own intuition, or aren't even sure *if* we're intuitive.

ACCESSING INTUITIVE EXPERIENCE

The experience of intuition is especially difficult to speak about, often having the quality of 'I know but can't explain *how* I know.' This ineffable, **non-discursive** quality can lead to so much confusion and doubt; if we don't understand intuition and have no good framework for recognizing what it is, then we are much more likely to dismiss it—and the intuitive voice goes unheard or ignored. That's why I believe it is so important to allow ourselves to really think about what intuition is and to base our attitudes about intuition on our lived experience of it.

With our limited conceptual structures for explaining intuition, firsthand experience is invaluable. But, because it happens below the threshold of consciousness (meaning, it's subconscious), we don't generally catch ourselves in the act of intuiting. Instead, we tend to know intuition in terms of its content, and even that can be difficult to parse out. We might be aware that there is something to know, without quite knowing what that is. And even when the content—the outcome of intuiting—is clear, the sequence of how we have come to that awareness is usually hazy at best. So, to know about intuitive experience, we have to look inward, through the filtering mechanisms of thoughts, beliefs, and assumptions, to access direct, inner awareness. And for that access, we can look to the practice of phenomenology.

Phenomenology is the study of what happens (*-ology*, meaning 'the study of' or 'having to do with' + phenomenon, meaning 'a fact or event' or 'what exists'). In phenomenological studies, experience is primary. But recognizing that what happens is impossible to capture except by the person who's experiencing it, phenomenologists ask all kinds of sub-questions. Things like: Who's asking?

And, who's reporting on these experiences? Questions of what a 'self' is arise here, and now we're halfway to metaphysics and what we ultimately believe is the nature of the universe. We'll get into those questions later in the book. But for now, let's focus on how phenomenology can get at the way we experience intuition.

As a research method, phenomenology lets us study direct inner experience by starting with what people actually experience. Rather than fitting the experience into an already-established category, it tries to bracket out theories or concepts (even though what we think and believe always helps structure what we understand to be happening). Phenomenology attempts to do away with the structuring effect of language and concepts to focus on firsthand experience—before interpretation, assessment, or judgment and before assigning any feelings to the experience.

In the 1990s, phenomenological researcher Dr. Claire Petitmengin set out to observe people in the moment of intuitive experience. Motivated by the lack of language available to describe the physical, sensory, and emotional experience of intuition, Petitmengin's team designed a study to catch people in the intuitive moment. Using research methods that strip away narrative, cognitive, and analytic content, they encouraged the subjects to find their own vocabulary for describing their experiences.

The study found that a vast majority of intuitive experiences involve a consistent set of four features: a letting go, connecting with the intuitive content, listening, and capturing. These are not necessarily sequential phases; they might all occur at once. But they're all present in intuitive experience, or the intuitive mode.

LETTING GO: Some aspects of intuitive experience are felt distinctly in the body. 'Letting go' might appear with a somatic signature (a **tell**), like a change in physical posture, the rate of breath slowing down, or heightened sensations throughout the body, like feelings of spaciousness around the head. This is a moment of relaxing into the experience, where the person's attention shifts inward; to the body rather than to the thoughts.

CONNECTING: Next, there's a sense of connection, where the person's awareness expands, relaxes, and sort of drifts off into a larger sphere. In this moment, attention becomes both panoramic and more discriminating at the same time. We might catch ourselves in a flow state, feeling more connected, but not attached. Connected to what? To something greater than oneself. To a unified field of consciousness, beyond individual consciousness, beyond time and space.

LISTENING: Then there is the arrival of the intuitive content itself—some idea, understanding, hunch, insight, or whatever it is. Participants in Petitmengin's study described how intuitive content "surges forth with a leap, unexpectedly, out of our control."[7] Within a state of receptive awareness, it can feel like the experience happens *to* us. After all, intuition is typically receptive, not active.

CAPTURING: And finally, there's the post-intuitive moment, when the intuiting person either accepts the awareness and stays open to unfolding its meaning and significance, or else chases it away (whether unintentionally because they've tried to capture the experience in words too soon, or on purpose, by rejecting the intuitive content). At the moment of intuition, we have a choice. We can stay with its arising, letting it appear to us, and then decide to trust what we now know...or not.

The phases of intuition described by this phenomenological study show that even though the experience is subjective and the range of intuitive tells vast, intuitive experiences follow a similar pattern, no matter who is experiencing it. The similarity of these signals complexifies the idea that intuition is *completely* subjective. Yes, intuition arrives to people differently, and we each have our own unique relationship to it, but the general character is similar across different people's experiences.

Petitmengin also found that people's attitude and beliefs affect how they relate to their intuitive experience. Those who are ready and receptive tend to experience intuition more easily than those who are resistant. This second group may still experience intuition, but at a higher threshold, sometimes layered over with emotions or inner dialogue that acts as a buffer or barrier to intuitive moments. We see this in real life: Higher threshold folks might only hear from their intuition in emergency situations or when it really counts.

For me, one of the most important findings of this study is that it's possible to prepare yourself for the intuitive moment, through a process of what Petitmengin calls "emptying out." In later chapters, we talk about cultivating this receptive awareness and what it takes to relax into and trust the experience, to be in flow, and to not let our thoughts or expectations interfere with it.

FEATURES OF INTUITIVE EXPERIENCE

When we start from the phenomenology of intuition—the lived experience of intuition—what can we learn about intuition on its own terms? In other words, what are the characteristics of the intuitive mode? What makes it intuition and not something else?

The intuitive mode is present, engaged, curious, receptive, and aware. And maybe more than a way of knowing, intuition is a way of *being*. When we are intuitive, we engage with a particular way of being in the world, of being in relation to our world. As far as how it *feels* to be in the intuitive mode, there are some characteristics we can point to. It feels like a flow state or receptive awareness. There's often a 'tell.' And it's immediate, bypassing conscious awareness.

Petitmengin's phenomenological study gave us a solid ground to describe the intuitive mode. In what follows, I outline six more aspects of intuitive experience that help us round out our understanding. Read on to see how intuition is holistic, non-discursive, personal (embodied) and transpersonal. It's oriented to possibility and can bring sudden insight about the present or future. And it can look—and feel—diverse, across a spectrum of experience, including ESP and psi.

EMBODIED

Often, intuition expresses through embodied sensations, rather than thought or feeling. We experience intuition in the body through the gut, with butterflies or chills, and by innumerable other tells.

A tell is a personal, embodied signal that alerts us to intuitive experience. It may be a subtle shift, like a deepening or slowing of breath, or it may be dramatic, like a sudden gasp or feeling like you need to gulp air. I have heard it called "ding! ding!" like inner alarm bells going off. There are probably as many unique tells as there are people.

The key is to learn *your* tells, so that you know when a sensation or fleeting feeling has meaning as intuitive experience—or not. Most of us ignore these tells in the moment. We might recognize, in hindsight, that something was meaningful. If we're lucky, we realize: "So that's what that was about!" Not: "Oops I should have listened."

Intuitive tells can arise in any area of the body. Some of the diverse tells I've heard of include sneezes, shivers, goosebumps, headaches, eye twitches, and cold feet (literally!). 'Gut feelings' are a whole category of intuitive tell.ᵛ Gut feelings are a euphemism, but they are also completely literal.

Some people register a particular taste when intuition hits (a tell that's sometimes called clairgustance). My friend Mike has an olfactory tell (clairalience): He smells lavender when something is good, right, or true and eggs (sulphur) when something isn't right. (Isn't that cool?!) These kinds of tells don't necessarily tell us *what* we need to know, but they act like an attention bell, ringing to alert us that we should pay attention. Ding, ding!

But of course, not every stomach ache or sneeze is a signal. Not every whiff of apple pie is an intuitive alert. And not every intuitive experience has an embodied accompaniment at all.

It's important to validate intuitive experiences that have no noticeable physiological correlate. Sometimes, there's no indicator. You just know. My own intuition is like this: it usually comes in the form of "just knowing"—aka clairsentience, or 'clear knowing.' No tell to speak of.

Clairsentient experiences are especially hard to describe because they are so subtle. And while in retrospect I can often point to an experience and identify it as intuitive, sometimes, in the moment, it's unclear. For example, a person I haven't thought of in a while floats through my awareness. It may arrive as a thought, such as "I wonder how so-and-so is doing?" or it may be an impression, like suddenly and for a very brief moment I am wondering about

---

v   Gut feelings, hunches, and other instinctual, embodied sensations are so ordinary to human experience that Rupert Sheldrake considers *them* the sixth sense and gives another name to psychic intuition—the seventh sense.

so-and-so. Maybe a picture of them or a memory flashes through my mind. And then, that person gets on the same bus as me, calls me on the phone, is at the restaurant I go to for lunch, etc.

Tells can be really subtle. And even when there's nothing to point to—no location in the body, no physical indicator—there is usually a *something*. A subtle sense of chills, sitting up straighter, a sense of expansion in the torso, or something else that tells us intuition is active.

IMMEDIATE

The experience of intuition usually feels sudden, spontaneous, direct, and/or immediate. This is probably because intuitive experience—at the moment of intuition—doesn't filter through thoughts or assumptions. At least not at first. That's why it sometimes gets called unmediated. Intuition's immediacy makes it seem sudden, but it doesn't always occur in the way a lightbulb goes off. It might not have the rush or shock that 'sudden' conveys.

Another way of thinking about the immediacy is in the sense used by philosopher Henri Bergson. He described intuition as a method or way of entering what he called "intellectual sympathy:" becoming one with an object of awareness.

In other words, without the mediating barriers of the conscious, rational mind, we can share consciousness with an idea, concept, or piece of information. In the intuitive moment, we *become one* with the thing we're perceiving. We literally resonate with or as the thing we are intuiting. This happens when we let our analytic guard down (in this case, a good thing!) and let the information, desire, understanding, meaning, or whatever content bubble up and come forth in awareness.

Sometimes intuition's immediacy happens because it has been processed below the threshold of consciousness. All of that processing arises (or seems to arise) to conscious awareness all at once, suddenly. You know how in math class you're supposed to show your work? With intuition, that's impossible. The intuitive mode often doesn't show its work at all. We *just* know. The answer, the understanding, the vision, it's just there. As if out of nowhere. This makes us want to trace the source, hence all the speculation and desire for explanation, and the draw to think of it as 'given'.

The unmediated nature of intuition is also why we hear about intuition being the way to know those things that are most difficult to put into any kind of language or concept. Ineffable qualities like the nature of reality are only ever accessed through non-discursive, transpersonal, intuitive means.

CERTAIN

Intuitive content tends to arrive with an affect, or aura, of certainty—a quality of being 'given'—that brings with it a feeling of confidence in the knowing. For unexplainable and not rationalizable reasons, we just know, and we feel sure about it.[vi] Certainty is most notable in aha moments and in the strength of conviction known as mothers' intuition. It might feel like a compulsion we must follow, like quickly getting out of the way of an impending accident. Or it can be a subtle but insistent, nagging feeling that reminds you over and over that a relationship is harmful and needs to be ended. This

---

vi Note that I'm talking about certainty in the intuitive experience itself; not the doubting or over-thinking that often happens right after.

certainty is an asset, especially when the intuitive content is surprising or asking us to act contrary to conventional wisdom.

Intuition's characteristic certainty occurs because it arises from within, so it can feel as though we've always known the content. The trick with intuitive certainty is that it can feel quite different from the certainty we expect from thinking or when we come to know something by figuring it out step-by-step. This quality of *just knowing* is a valid experience, but it can be very hard to trust when there's nothing at all to point to. When nothing discernible has happened, not even butterflies or a nose twitch, it's easy to gaslight ourselves out of the experience—and into thinking that nothing has happened.

We might think about the ways that we do and do not trust our inner experience when it comes with a physical correlation (as with felt sensation) versus when it doesn't (as intuition often does not). When an intuitive experience is associated with a physical tell, we might be more likely to trust it. This theme is consistent throughout our culture: we tend to trust as real and true what we can see with our own eyes, but not necessarily so with our inner sight.

The experience of certainty (the feeling or vibe that often comes with intuitive experience) doesn't necessarily mean that it's correct, as in Absolutely True. Something might be true right now, or true for you in this moment, and yet not true objectively. We'll talk more about how to discern intuition's validity in later chapters.

HOLISTIC

Intuitive experience is holistic in that the whole of a thing can be known or understood intuitively, all at once. Intuitive content tends to present itself as complete,[vii] which makes it useful for perceiving the whole picture, or a bigger picture, or for recognizing a broader scope of choices than you're able to think of. Sometimes, an idea comes fully formed and complete, which also explains why it feels like it's come out of nowhere (and, often, suddenly). But what's likely happening is that the intuitive mode creates meaning by synthesis: It synthesizes clues and recognizes patterns, drawing from multiple directions or sources, such as our own memories, clues from the environment, inner awareness, and unseen or transpersonal sources. We might even be pulling from the past and the future at the same time.

This holistic character of the intuitive mode is not linear. Information can be mixed up, jumbled all together, or out of order. And this makes it hard to know where our knowing comes from, especially when the whole of a thing can sometimes make more sense than the parts.

Intuition is also holistic in that the experience of intuiting can involve any or all of the intellect, the emotions, the physical body, and the subtle (energy) body. Even though intuition isn't the same as thinking, nor is it a feeling, it can register as either of those things. A thought floats through our mind. Or we have an insistent desire. Or we experience an embodied sensation. Intuitive experience might transit through any of the ordinary five senses, or it might bypass these senses so we get a hit of 'extra-sensory perception.'

So when we can't discern *how* we know, it might be because the mind, emotions, and body are all involved, often simultaneously. Intuition recruits the body, mind, and psyche as an integrated

---

[vii] This idea is from Jung back in 1971.

(holistic) system. And, although it's experienced by an individual person, that individual exists in a holistic context, in relationship with human and non-human others in complex, dynamic systems of interrelatedness. We are all connected, after all! On the level of consciousness, plants, animals, and the spirit world are in a communicative relationship with each other and with humans who are open to receiving these communicative offerings. Connections between and through all of these aspects of the (holistic) self make intuition possible.

Back in the day, when it was even more taboo to talk about inner experience, the word 'holistic' used to refer to any version of a modality that included spirituality, energy, or the unseen aspects of experience—anything more than the material, physical facets. For example, holistic *education* goes beyond the intellectual to include social-emotional and sometimes even the psycho-spiritual aspects to learning. In other words, things you can't measure. Likewise, holistic *medicine* is an approach to health and healthcare that recognizes and supports all aspects of a person, again including their psycho-spiritual well-being, and possibly making use of modalities of diagnosis or care that are unconventional or untestable.

So, when I describe intuitive experience as holistic, I'm not only trying to communicate that intuition involves the whole person. It does. But I'm also pointing to a characteristic of intuitive experience that draws on unseen resources.

Once we begin to accept and recognize the holistic nature of intuitive experience, we can better accept intuitive experience as it is. We can stop looking for its parts, its beginning and end, or expecting it to arrive as a thought versus an emotional tone versus an idea. The components might be impossible to parse, but we don't have to, if we let it be intuitive.

TRANSPERSONAL

Intuitive experience puts us in contact with a **dimension** (or more accurately, dimension*s*) of experience beyond the personal. And that's what the word *transpersonal* means. It signifies the more—or the *moreness*—that exists beyond what we normally recognize as our individual realm of experience. Without necessarily defining the specifics of that moreness (which gets interpreted as god, spirit, energy, love, or something else, depending on what you believe), we might think of it as the collective dimension of experience or the creative, metaphysical forces that some simply call *the unseen realm*.

Intuition is a transpersonal experience in (at least) two ways. One, intuition itself is made possible by transcending the ordinary limitations of the boundaries of time, space, and individual consciousness. And two, we typically become aware of transpersonal stuff through intuitive experiences.

We generally experience our connection to the transpersonal dimensions through bonds, relationships, and transfers of energy. And some of the explanations for how and why such ('non-ordinary') experiences are possible lead to a metaphysics that is very much like spiritual insight. For example, the concept (or awareness, or understanding, or experience) that individual humans are but a tiny piece of a huge, vast universe and yet at the same time we have agency to shape our lived experience. Or the idea that information can be known across time and space (four dimensions among other—unseen and unknown—dimensions), and the related notion that there is an undifferentiated awareness we can sometimes tap into to access information *beyond* the dimensions of time and space. These transpersonal concepts are explainable by theoretical physics, and they are also spiritual, mystical insights.

As a transpersonal experience, intuition provides a sense of coherence and meaning and gives rise to the feeling that we are connected to a collective unity that is greater than the one we can see.

The individual person is still important, though. When we understand intuition as transpersonal, it becomes easier to see how it works as a mode of communication between the conscious and unconscious mind or between the individual and collective aspects of self, beyond and between the boundaries of any one person. In other words, intuition is an experience of resonance that lets the individual perceive on the level of the greater, universal whole.

While each of us experience or express intuition individually, intuitive experience is made possible by entering into communion with a field of yet-unmanifest potential. Intuitive experience is an interaction between the individual self, the depths of the personal and transpersonal well of experience, and the vast expanse of collective and universal consciousness.

Connected to both psychology and philosophy, transpersonal *theory* draws from several of the world's wisdom traditions, especially Buddhism, Hinduism, Taoism, and shamanic traditions from diverse Indigenous lineages. Not coincidentally, these traditions seem to have a much easier time accepting intuition as meaningful; it's baked into their worldview. For example, in the Vedic tradition from India, knowledge is understood to be pre-existent: There is an already-existing, subjectively verifiable knowledge that humans have forgotten but which is available to be known—if the mind can become receptive to it.

The wise cultures that evolved these systems can also account for the perception of energy itself. They accept and acknowledge that energy moves throughout the world, including through our bodies. These lineages have language for energy anatomy that describes how energy moves within and through the embodied form, and they have a concept of mind-body nonduality that contrasts with the rationalist understanding that the mind and body are separate.

By describing intuitive experience as transpersonal, we set ourselves up for trusting inner experiences of psychic and extended consciousness and valuing that the category of experience we call 'intuition' includes so-called non-ordinary ways of knowing.

NON-DISCURSIVE

With intuition, it's possible to know something even if we can't put that knowledge into words. Often, our intuitive experiences are not concrete enough to put the frame of language around. No words. No context. No frame. No shape. This may be because the perception is so subtle, you're not sure how to put it into words. Or it might simply be that the experience is happening outside the domain of language, ideas, and concepts. This quality of not relating to words or language, is called non-discursive.

The non-discursive quality of intuitive experience is why you get people saying, "*I just know*." You don't know *how* you know; you *just know*. In this way, intuitive experiences are often beyond intangible, they are un-speak-about-able. There are no words or concepts to adequately explain what's happening.

Many experiences besides intuitive ones aren't speakable in words or concepts. It's difficult to speak about intuition the same way it can be difficult to say what feelings feel like. Or to tell someone about our dreams, or about what we experience in meditation. When we try to explain a dream, it can end up sounding like "...I was in a cave, but it was also my teenage bedroom—it looked like my friend's room, but in the dream it was mine—and a rabbit hopped out of the closet and it looked me in the eye, and I thought to myself, that horse has eight legs..." You've had dreams like that, right?

There are other modes of consciousness as well where things don't make sense in the way they normally do and that don't lend themselves to language. Non-discursive awareness is what we're actively seeking through meditation and other contemplative practices, where we work to get into a wordless state on purpose, to experience what there is beyond—or between—thoughts. And through psychedelic trips where we intentionally usher our consciousness into non-ordinary states, to perceive things beyond the boundaries of space-time. In those states, we can often sense colours, shapes, and patterns, and watch energies shift and move in ways that we might not be able to explain in words.

Non-discursive doesn't mean it doesn't make sense though. Being able to put something into language doesn't make it more valuable. It's just that there's a gap between experience and representing that experience through language.

But because intuitive experience is non-discursive, we don't have a great deal of shared language for communicating about our experiences with intuition, leading to all the different ways intuition gets interpreted, defined, and described. The non-discursive quality of intuition is also why skeptics might want to dismiss intuitive experience. Like, if you can't explain it, how can it be real? And this is not just about communicating to others. This gap applies to how we express our experience to ourselves. (Our internalized, inner skeptic gets quite activated by non-discursivity.)

Language does help structure what we know and what we believe. It can also reveal what we *already* believe. But modern, rational people make a classic mistake. We equate naming with knowing and assume that if something can't be put into words, we can't know it. Of course, this is untrue, since we recognize that non-discursive experiences like wonder, love, and joy are very much real, even if they're hard to communicate directly through language.

It's like with a piece of music or a poem; we can know that it has evoked something, even if we can't say what. Likewise, we might not be able to communicate the experience of seeing a double rainbow discursively, but someone else can know more or less what we mean when they hear us gasp in awe or say "wow" over and over again. We're more likely to be able to interpretative dance about that experience than write an essay about it. Maybe we could paint it or turn to some other non-verbal expression. Remember studying poetry in school and learning about symbols and metaphor? Poets—and all of us sometimes—rely on metaphor when we want to communicate what we really mean because words and concepts can never fully express the wholeness or complexity of a thing. This is because the experience is non-discursive.

With any of these experiences, there's a lot going on under the surface of consciousness, and we won't always have access to the process that lets us arrive at the knowledge or understanding. We know it has meaning. But the meaning is not necessarily something we can define well enough to talk or even think about.

Intuitive knowledge, information, or understanding might not even be comprehensible to the intellect. It's more likely to communicate through symbolic language. So if it's non-discursive and we can't know it through ideas or words or concepts or any of the usual ways we consider valid, what are we left with? The inner experience of intuiting; known through a vast, holistic array of subjective tells, individual and collective symbols, images, and feelings.

SO, WHAT IS INTUITION?

All of these features of intuitive experience point us to consider intuition as an experience, a mode, or even a relationship between aspects of consciousness that communicate with each other. I've always liked a definition for intuition given by writer Annie Devereaux, who explains intuition as "a state of communication, individually expressed as an interaction between the conscious and unconscious mind, through the medium of dreams, visions, and feelings."[8]

Individually expressed refers to the way that each individual has their own ways of experiencing, recognizing, and interpreting intuition. We've started to explore how individual knowers will have their unique, subjective experiences of intuition, based on who they are, what they believe, etc. *Interaction between the conscious and unconscious mind* helps explain why intuition seems to come out of the blue and why it can offer up unconventional or unexpected content; some part of ourselves—a part we usually don't have much awareness of—does the perceiving (whether it's accessing new content, recognizing patterns, or coming to a new understanding) and that content arises to the conscious, rational, language-oriented part of ourselves for interpretation, language, and meaning. (Keep in mind, this interaction is not just one-directional; as we'll explore later, the known and the knower act on each other.)

On its own terms, intuition is a holistic, embodied, non-discursive mode of consciousness. It connects us to a more expansive sense of reality, where the personal, individual self comes into contact with transpersonal dimensions of consciousness, letting us know—without containing that experience within the limiting effects of language, cognition, or analysis. If we're too attached to interpreting our experience as this-means-that, that-means-this, we risk misinterpreting intuitive experience, or missing it all together. Remember, things that are non-discursive often get lumped in with things that aren't real. And although it can be difficult or even impossible to express this stuff in words, with practice, we can learn to trust that *we do know*. We can know intuition as a lived experience; through the body and its sensorium and through extra-sensory perception, an experience of resonance and connection.

Chapter 3
HOW DOES INTUITION WORK?

WHAT IS INTUITION?

People always seem to want to know the *how* of intuition. They ask, "How does it work?" And, "Is this stuff proven?" Now it's time to answer the question: how is it even possible to know without knowing how you know?

We tend to be aware of the intuitive mode, the intuitive process, when it produces an outcome—some content, decision, or understanding that appears in our awareness, seemingly fully formed: sudden, direct, and whole. But how the heck did it get there? If I have psychic experiences or perceive energy or access precognitive awareness, then what do I need to understand to have those intuitive experiences make sense? In other words, what makes intuitive experience even possible? This chapter will start to answer that.[i]

I'm just going to say this at the outset: It's a mistake to try to understand intuition (what it is, how to cultivate it) by approaching it with the assumptions and modalities that belong to analysis. Linear, rational, analytic logic is generally unsuited to making sense of intuition. As we've learned, intuition is holistic, immediate, embodied, transpersonal, and non-discursive, and relies on dynamics of unseen energy. So, if our goal is to understand

---

[i] As for is it proven, the answer is yes...and also no. There have been many studies that test, measure, and confirm non-ordinary consciousness and psychic intuition. The validity of experiences like telepathy, future-knowing, and nonlocal or remote seeing are well established. When scientists are committed to an open and curious inquiry about what's possible—such as in the field of nonlocal, conscious awareness—they can theorize and often confirm its existence. In scientific practice, what starts as fringe often makes its way to the mainstream. Research institutes like the International Consciousness Research Laboratories (ICRL, formerly Princeton Engineering Anomalies Lab) and the Institute of Noetic Sciences (IONS) have published numerous successful scientific studies that disrupt the modern Western narrative about consciousness and prove the existence of psychic phenomena.

intuition on its own terms, our approach will have to be a little different.

On its own terms, intuitive experience is best explained as a function of relational, contextual, energetic awareness. It's not analytic or rational, but is a whole other way to experience and produce knowledge. Whereas the analytic mode takes things apart to understand them and requires that we label, categorize, and name each part of a thing as part of the process of knowing it, the intuitive mode orients to wholes, systems, and dynamic movement. Intuition senses meaning rather than always articulating it in words and concepts. It produces knowledge through recognizing patterns and resonance.

Taking our lead from the intuitive mode itself, it's not my intent to achieve some specific, absolute explanation for the mechanism of intuition. We shouldn't have to conceptualize, analyze, or understand intuition in the same ways we need to understand construction engineering, nutritious recipes, or how the Earth's water cycles work to bring about weather patterns. Remember when I said this wasn't a how-to book, it's a why-to? That applies to this chapter too. It's important not to get too consumed by the requirement for scientific proof or validity. Wanting that proof in the first place is a characteristic of a scientific-materialist approach to knowledge that I'd like us to resist, at least for the duration of this chapter. In practice, expecting truth and certainty interferes with intuitive experience, let alone with our understanding of what it is and what that says about ourselves, consciousness, and the ways of the world. Instead, my goal is to contextualize, not necessarily define; to create a nest of context into which we can weave, or layer, ways of understanding—of intuition, and ultimately, of ourselves.

WHAT IS INTUITION?

Regardless of the mechanics of intuitive experience, what's more important to me is, how do we cultivate trust in our intuitive experience? And knowing what we believe intuition *is* contributes to developing that trust.

If we want to cultivate, or even just understand, intuition, it can help our confidence to know that what we're dealing with is real, which can be a challenge. What we understand about the nature of the world tends to be structured by the dominant paradigms of the day. And today, that's a scientific and mechanistic framework, with a baked-in assumption that everything can be rationally justified. I think its helpful if we can tend to those parts of ourselves that have learned to doubt and are skeptical of even our own experiences. These parts feel reassured by an explanation, so I'm going to provide a version of one here. Note that some of this is 'proven' and some isn't. I'm asking you to suspend your desire for concrete validation, and instead to be with and inhabit the framework I present here. Try it on.

We're socialized to want proof. We want to know that what we know—and what we are—is acceptable.

And so, if an explanation helps our brains get on board with accepting intuition as a powerful ally, let's do it. Let's explain intuition. Let's try to understand intuition.

An important part of the project of understanding intuition on its own terms is looking for metaphors that might replace the mechanistic metaphysics that uphold linear, predictable, binary reason. I believe there is tremendous value in allowing ourselves to consider the metaphysics that let intuition make sense. So, some of my intent behind framing intuition as a function of resonance and connection is the way that it expands how we understand ourselves and our nature as interconnected beings, alive in the world. In other words, intuition on its own terms shows us who we are.

It's all so meta: To understand intuition on its own terms, we need an intuitive, holistic, transpersonal way of thinking about consciousness and about experience. Whatever metaphors we choose have to account for the various types of intuitive experience that exist, including energy sensitivity, implicit knowing, and nonlocal intuition. Dance, flow, and garden are just some of the woo-friendly metaphors that might work here. These evoke intuition's transpersonal, holistic, immediate, non-discursive nature, and gesture to the living systems that comprise our reality.

But in this chapter, I'm going to suggest we use a quantum metaphor.

A quantum framework is an obvious option for speculating about how intuition works, because of the involvement of nonlocal knowing, energetic sensitivity, and the entanglement of consciousness. It begins with the assumption that the world is composed of energy, and that energy carries information. In other words, energy is not 'just' energy. It's information. As physicists tell us, energy has shape and pattern, which carry information.

We can also refer to this framework as akashic, in the lineage of Ervin Laszlo and other teachers who use this language to describe how we are all connected through fields of energy.[9] In the quantum (or akashic) dimension, *everything* is inherently interconnected. The quantum field (or quantum vacuum) is an energetic field that is the foundation of, and gives rise to, form. As a field, it is present everywhere, so it's always unified. This is the basis of entanglement and what allows entanglement to exist. It is the ground of all being.

The quantum metaphor points to the possibility of nonlinear space-time and offers a logic of indeterminacy and potential, of not-yet-defined, where uncertainty and probability are the basis of what happens. From this perspective, intuition is an experience of resonance that relies on the potential for human consciousness to transmit and perceive fields and vibrations of energy, when received by a self-aware, receptive subject. The metaphor nudges us to wrap our heads around both/and logic and what that means for 'truth' and validity—beyond either/or. It encourages us to realize that nondual entanglement (ultimate connection) is the context in which the living systems of human and non-human consciousness are embedded.

With this quantum, akashic, 'woo' framework, we have a foundation for understanding intuition on its own terms.

DIMENSIONALITY

The quantum (akashic) metaphor[ii] relies on a basic hypothesis about the universe: that it is comprised of multiple dimensions. While we're very used to thinking in 4D—three dimensions of space + time; call it space-time, if you will—quantum theorists make sense of anomalies in the universe by projecting at least nine functioning dimensions that comprise our reality (and some suggest there are many more). These multiple dimensions of reality are said to coexist in a holographic form, where every aspect of reality exists on every dimension or plane. Taken together, all of

---

ii   Note that I'm insisting on calling it a metaphor because I'm not a physicist and don't actually know about this from a scientific point of view. Rather than making a *scientific* case here, I'm using the ideas as a philosopher; to build a framework or perspective.

the dimensions comprise the akasha, the unified field in which everything—absolutely everything—exists.

This framework suggests that out beyond 4D space-time is a domain of unseen dimensions in which all matter is undivided, flowing in a universal flux—a quantum soup or akashic field. Scientist and philosopher David Bohm called this domain the *implicate order*. Here, I'll also call it the *unseen dimension* (and sometimes, *akashic field*). This is the domain[iii] of potentiality, where everything is entangled, instantly interconnected; where there is no form, just consciousness. In the akashic field, time and space unfold together in a self-organizing whole. Every thing and every event occur together, simultaneously, already entangled or enfolded and nested within itself.

The implicate order applies to both matter (substance) and consciousness. Everything is enfolded into itself and each other, and as things become manifest (which not everything does), they emerge from this cosmic soup. As Amit Goswami writes, "Form is manifested in a specific way when a possibility is chosen and collapsed into actuality—manifest reality."[10] In this sense, the physical form of a thing is not distinct from its energetic form.

Are you still with me? Think of a spectrum of existence, from potential to actual. Everything is energy. It's all already in existence, though not necessarily manifest—more like on a spectrum of manifestation, from subtle to dense. On the dense end, matter is coherent and manifest enough to be perceived or physically sensed. On the subtle end is the vast, vibrating, pulsating soup of potential that we generally don't perceive at all.

---

iii The language of "domains" comes from Amit Goswami.

All things exist in the multidimensional multiverse—at least they exist in a state of potential. This is why we can say that things are both discrete AND entangled. The closer things are to being material and solid, the more discrete—or specific—they are. The more solid, the more boundaried. This is true for objects as well as for ideas and intuitive content (thoughts, dreams, visions, etc.).

The concept of multiple dimensions of existence is not recent. Many ancient spiritual traditions propose the idea of multiple planes or states of reality, including the physical, mental, astral, and causal. All of these are always present, even when we're unaware of them because we typically focus our attention on local, 4D space-time. After all, our consciousness is attuned to perceive a limited spectrum of information.

The unseen, akashic dimensions exist in a range beyond our usual perceptual abilities, so we don't typically perceive them. But while it's impossible to perceive all of these dimensions with the sensory tools we have, we shouldn't assume that the unseen dimensions aren't real or relevant. Instead, we should understand that everything we can see, smell, touch, or perceive with our senses may be only a small slice of what exists—or could exist.

ENTANGLEMENT, AKA CONNECTION

A key idea about the akasha is the innate wholeness and interconnectedness of the universe. Here's how that works.

We tend to think that the world is made up of matter and energy, but the quantum framework adds another layer: when we look very closely, at the atomic scale, matter *is* energy!

Quanta are the smallest known packets of energy in the universe.[11] Quantum *entanglement* refers to the way that systems that intra-act in any way, remain connected; even after they've been moved apart, even by massive distance. Einstein and his contemporaries reckoned that entanglement was nonsense (he called it "spooky action at a distance"), since that would mean particles are basically communicating faster than the speed of light, which at the time, was thought to be impossible. But guess what!?

The current science of nonlocality tells us that paired electrons are affected together, even if they are no longer linked spatially. Nonlocality demonstrates "the fundamental interconnection of everything at the quantum level such that faster-than-the-speed-of-light communication/interaction is implied between subatomic particles separated in space/time by vast distances."[12] In other words, quanta remain non-locally entangled. Particles remain entangled, no matter how great the distance, and this remains true not only for super-small quantum things. All things are entangled. All things are instantly interconnected. This applies to physical objects, to consciousness, to everything. Because everything is, at its root, quantum.

Whether in the manifest world, or in the unseen dimensions, the very nature of life is entanglement, connection, interaction. After all, "all things are what they are through their interactions."[13] As an example on the material plane, we can consider any plant, taking in carbon dioxide from the air animals have exhaled, and using sunlight to create its physical form (the substance of its leaves, roots, flowers). The plant then releases the oxygen we need to live. This is **intra-active** respiration that goes beyond interdependence; it's synergistic, with the physical structures of plants serving as food for other life forms that also breathe, and on and on.

In the akashic domain, outside of space and time, entanglement means that information can come through the unified field, into individuals' perception, bypassing time and space. Each unit of information overlaps with the past and with the future at the same time (because it is simultaneous), and no signals or mediation are required for this communication to take place.[14] In other words, it's *immediate*.

We can use the idea of entanglement to start to explain how it's possible to know things outside of space and time, how it's possible to know another's mind, or how it's possible to foresee or foreknow without any discernible clues. In the quantum field (or, akashic dimension), things are not separable, including the object and subject of knowledge.

ENERGETIC SENSITIVITY AND THE EMBODIED SELF

It's no coincidence that vibe is a common synonym for intuition. But there's a need to clarify our vocabulary, because when it comes to intuition, vibe can mean multiple things at once. You've likely heard slogans appealing to 'good vibes,' evoking the Beach Boys and the flower-power hippie culture of the 1960s and 70s. Back then, vibe referred mostly to mood or affect; a feeling. But the hippies were also—knowingly or not—talking about energy. Because after all, what creates an atmosphere or mood that other people can pick up on, that can linger in a room, even after the people who were arguing have left it? Patterns of vibrations.

Merriam-Webster defines vibes as "a distinctive feeling or quality, capable of being sensed"—sensible but intangible. Vibes are an experience of shared resonance between parts of ourselves, between people, between anything really. As a synonym for intuition, 'vibes' makes sense, since we're talking about something that involves energy and emotion, as well as interpersonal, interconnected, psychic forms of affect.

We know vibrations through their movement; we sense their flow and oscillation through resonance. That's why 'yes' vibes feel different from 'no' vibes, and why we can register what we want (and don't want) through tells like tingles, a sense of expansion, innervation, rushes, etc. This sensitivity is a fundamental feature of organism. Of course, we can't do this without a body. Resonance is a physical, sometimes sensible, way our bodies register and relay connectedness, part of the human sensory system.

It's not radical to say that humans resonate to vibrations. Our bodies are equipped to register a range of wavelengths that let us know about, and communicate with, our surroundings and each other. Light, heat, and sound waves are all examples of information carried on vibrations. Brain wave readings (EEGs) have demonstrated vibrations registered in the brain that align with particular states of consciousness. Some are responsible for the deep relaxation we experience in sleep; others correspond to a trippy, psychedelic set of experiences. These waves are created by coherent, aka synchronized, patterns of electrons; neurons firing in synchronization, moving together.

Other animals generate and perceive vibrations, too, through various, diverse electromagnetic capabilities. Eels can perceive objects via self-generated electric fields, even in the dark depths of the ocean.[15] Birds'[16] and butterflies' migrations are guided by internalized, electromagnetic 'maps.'

As living organisms, we are all made up of many dimensions of consciousness, including instinct, affect, biochemical responses, unconscious and subconscious layers. Resonating to our surroundings, maintaining more or less porous boundaries, our bodies and minds register and transmit unseen energies through vibrations all the time. Embodiment is the vehicle through which we can experience our entangled, nondual reality.

HEART AS AN ORGAN OF PERCEPTION

Gut feelings are a particularly well-known way to refer to embodied resonance. They're generally recognized as having validity, even though the term has become a generic way to describe any bodily response beyond ordinary consciousness. The actual, physical gut is the gastrointestinal tract, a central channel of nerves that transmits information throughout the nervous system. And it doesn't just signal satiety and hunger; the gut can alert us to danger or anxiety even before the brain registers it. All kinds of emotion and information transit through the gut.

But did you know that the heart is an important organ of perception, too? Like the gut, the human heart is sensitive to informational content that arises from outside as well as from within (since these aren't separate or distinct, after all). Many of us know from experience about the heart's sensitivity to vibes. We feel the swell of emotion as a complex physical sensation—both the painful sensations of heartbreak and the expansive feelings of love. This isn't just metaphoric. We now know that the human heart is capable of transmitting and receiving vibrations and the information they carry, making it an important organ of perception and resonance.

The brain and heart both generate measurable electromagnetic fields, but the heart's is far larger than the brain's, possibly generating about 60 times more amplitude.[17] It turns out, the heart's electromagnetic field can be detected and measured several feet away from a person's body.[18]

The amplitude of the heart's field might be responsible for what we call empathic intuition, when we perceive a vibe, mood, or thought, as it arises in another person. Empathic intuition explains the intuitive resonance between parent and child or any people who love each other; in any open-hearted connection where awareness transfers without the need for language, intuitive channels are often more accessible.

Our collective understanding about the heart as an organ of perception continues to emerge. Studies suggest that the heart registers intuitive information a fraction before the brain does.[19] It's possible that the brain interferes with this transmission, cutting off awareness of it before we cognitively register intuitive content. The brain, trained over time to filter, judge, doubt, and critique, jumps on the experience before it reaches conscious awareness.

EXTRA-SENSORY PERCEPTION

The sixth sense is what we colloquially tend to call the capacity to perceive through resonance. For some reason, we seem to make a distinction between a sixth sense (something that is at least somewhat felt, or identifiable, like a gut feeling) and extra-sensory perception, when something is simply known, without any presence of a bodily feeling. But when we're talking about intuition as an embodied experience, what does *extra*-sensory mean?

Perception of vibrations is partly a matter of our sensory 'equipment.' We know that human eyes can only perceive a portion of the electromagnetic spectrum. (We call that the visual spectrum and name what we can see as 'light.') With sound, we know there is a much larger range than what we can perceive. Think about the high-pitched sounds dogs hear, but we don't. Dogs have a larger, more extended auditory range of perception. (For what it's worth, they have a far superior sense of smell, too.)

And there are other wavelengths that humans don't ordinarily perceive. In fact, most of the range of electromagnetic frequencies is unseeable by the naked eye. Radio, television, cell phones, and Wi-Fi are all examples of energies we only perceive with technologies and tools that help extend our range of perception.

But perception is also more than equipment; it's also partly a matter of how we direct our attention, how relaxed our nervous system is, what we expect to see or if we're hoping to see something in particular. Sometimes, if we're looking too hard rather than with a quality of receptive awareness, it constrains our perception. It's like looking at stars in a night sky: The more relaxed and receptive our attention, the more stars become apparent, while focusing deeply on one area causes most of the other stars to recede from our awareness—literally becoming more difficult to see.

By habit and convention, we exclude a lot of input, only allowing in a narrow band of what's available. The brain especially tends to filter out nonlocal energy (all that potential in the implicate order), since it doesn't even seem possible to perceive, even with the most sophisticated of tools. However, in non-ordinary states or in moments of intuitive flow, when we release the boundaries of convenience that allow us to get through the day in the 'seen' world, we can sometimes access this unseen reality.

Extra-sensory or non-ordinary perception (like telepathy, precognition, and clairvoyance) is possible because we also, always, co-exist in the transpersonal, multidimensional, invisible world just as much as in the material domain. We just don't usually pay attention to it! And because consciousness becomes such a matter of habit, if we only ever attend to mundane, 'ordinary' consciousness, that becomes the entirety of what we will ever perceive.

This is important: Our subjective experience of perception is somewhat unique. Who we are, how we are, what we believe, what we pay attention to, things we've learned in our lifetime, our inclinations, inhibitions, desires, etc., all contribute to how we perceive—in the outer world as well as in the inner and unseen worlds. Because humans are diverse, some people are naturally attuned to a wider spectrum. We also pay more attention to things we have strong associations to than things we're indifferent to. And, in turn, what we pay attention to tends to grow in importance. What all this means is that, to some extent, we can change the range of what we perceive.

This is true of all senses, really. While we tend to think of sensing as innate rather than learned, cultural variations show us that senses—and what we consider 'sensory' or 'sensible'—are indeed conditioned and can be cultivated. For example, I grew up knowing as a fact (!) that humans have five senses that more or less correspond to the holes in our heads (plus our skin). We tend to think of these senses as universal, but other cultures register senses differently. I'm thinking of the Anlo-Ewe of Western Africa, who recognize humans as having as many as 23 senses, including proprioception (the experience of our body in space, like knowing where to place your foot when walking) and the sensory experience of what foods feel like in the mouth.[20]

So calling some things 'sensory' and others 'extra-sensory' is a matter of convention and of culture. In a materially-oriented culture, we make certain assumptions about what counts as a 'sense.' But our assessment and categorizations can and should shift. Our culture is moving towards recognizing intuition as a sixth sense, and our science continues to demonstrate that most humans can perceive beyond the presumed five senses.[iv] One day, maybe it will become obvious that we have six (or seven or eight!) senses, and what's now called 'extra' sensory, will just be known as yet another range of sensory capacity.

CONSCIOUSNESS AND NONLOCAL INTUITION

While some intuitive perception is a function of electromagnetic resonance—our hearts-brains-guts are bundles of nerves that project and receive information from inside and outside the body—other intuitive experiences happen as a result of nonlocal communication beyond the space-time dimension. And to understand that we need to consider how we understand consciousness, beyond the physical body.

Countless theories exist for the what and how of consciousness. Thinking about consciousness is so difficult that scientists and philosophers just call it "the hard problem."[21] What makes the most sense to me is to consider that, ultimately, consciousness is what gets called the quantum field.

In common language, consciousness generally refers to our thoughts, feelings, and perceptions of inner and outer experience and our awareness of perceiving these. We can think of consciousness as an internalized map of the world. Its primary function is to create order so that we can perceive—and then make sense of—our surroundings and experiences. Consciousness sorts

---

iv   There are many studies I could cite here. In particular, check out the compelling research done by both IONS and the HeartMath institute.

content; registering details, creating memory, and acting as a filter, so we don't get overwhelmed by the enormous amount of input available to us.

Behind the question of what consciousness is, is a more basic question about mind and matter. We know a lot about neuroscience and the brain, yet still don't have consensus about consciousness. A rational-materialist framing says that the brain is responsible for consciousness, a result of material processes like neurons firing, biochemical influences, etc. This kind of explanation works well for machines or anything we can take apart and reassemble. But humans are organisms, not mechanisms. And yes, our neurons do fire and biochemistry affects our experience, but we're neither passive nor static nor discrete. We're electromagnetic, interconnected, and dynamic, and we have energetic fields (our aura) and nervous systems that participate in nonlocal coherence. So the materialist theory of consciousness doesn't reflect the complexity of what we experience.

But a recent theory[22] suggests that consciousness is a function of resonance. This theory suggests that resonance—i.e., synchronized vibrations—is responsible for consciousness, along with everything we know, and everything that is (!). Vibrations, it seems, are the foundation of physical reality in general, as well as our experience of it.

The resonance theory of consciousness posits that synchronized vibrations are central; not only to human consciousness but to all of physical reality. Every physical object vibrates and oscillates, even objects that appear to be stationary.[23] "Ultimately, all matter is just vibrations of various underlying fields."[24] When different oscillating things are close together for a time, they begin to vibrate in sync (a phenomenon called entrainment). This phenomenon applies to neurons in brains, fireflies gathering, the movement of the moon and the earth, and far more. This spontaneous self-organization is a manifestation of communication between entities—or, you could say, a manifestation of alignment and entanglement. The more synchronized these vibrations become, the more complex our connection with the world around us and the more sophisticated our consciousness.

Human bodies also emit (radiate) vibrations of energy. When our energy resonates with the wave form of information, that interaction makes it possible to know things, even across or beyond distance and time. Hence, nonlocal intuition.

Intuitive experience can happen because of resonance between conscious and unconscious aspects of our self or between individual and collective aspects. Either way, intuition is something that happens to and through us, as conscious, alive beings. Resonance depends on coherence, an alignment between ourselves—the perceiver—and whatever we're perceiving. The more coherent the emotional, attentional interest directed to the object of interest, the greater our access to the field of quantum, nonlocal information and so the greater the intuitive connection. This isn't the kind of knowing where we can ever take ourselves out of the equation; Intuition doesn't happen without an embodied, living knower who processes awareness and makes sense of what they know.

Before I started to understand resonance, entanglement, and the quantum theories that ground intuitive experience as a function of resonance, I used to imagine intuitive perception as being like a screen grab. All the information, knowledge, potentials are out there (somewhere!?) and for whatever reason, in some states of mind, we can capture a piece of that infinite awareness. We might imagine that some part of us stays connected to the akashic domain at all times, roaming the vast dimensions of transpersonal consciousness, where it perceives information, recognizes patterns, or gains understanding and then sometimes offers that content up to the conscious, rational, language-oriented mind for interpretation and meaning.

Now, I think of nonlocal intuitive experiences like dipping a toe into the implicate order—accessing a moment of resonance with, and as, the soup of infinite potential; connecting to a slice of information before it has become explicit.

Bohm explains that this toe-dipping connection is made possible because energy is not static but is a dynamic flux characterized by movement.[25] And this movement is not simply a fluid flow. It happens in jerks, leaps, and jumps; it's random and spontaneous; it can happen in any direction. Within this movement, it's thought that electrons make "virtual transitions"—they spread out and test the waters of shifts before changing orbit. These virtual transitions are temporary, but they still create a probability wave, so they have lasting impact. This might be one key to how we can perceive something intuitively, plucking it from the realm of potential, as it becomes manifest in the explicate world for a moment. The implicate has become explicit—actual—for a very brief time, and we picked up on it, resonated with it. (This also explains why there's some degree of uncertainty inherent with nonlocal intuition.)

SUBJECTIVE PERCEPTION

As we continue to discuss the 'logic' of intuition through themes like resonance, entanglement, and nonduality, this seems like a good time to remember that where we stand to look at the world—and the lens we use—changes what we can see. Maybe it seems obvious, but any aspect of reality or experience can be approached from any number of vantage points.

For example, think about the diverse ways to perceive a coastline.

From a distance, or on a map, coastlines seem distinct; more or less binary. There is the land, and there is the water. With distance, it's reasonable to perceive that at some definite point, the land ends and the water begins. That's how a coastline appears with the lens of objectivity.

But what do we see when we are *at* the coast or on the actual beach? What can we perceive from within the context of the beach itself? From that vantage point, we don't have the ability to see the shoreline in its totality, but a whole other range of perceptions do become available.

Up close, our senses perceive a whole other range of information. We might see patterns in the sand left by the waves, or by insects. We might notice that the sand is made up of particles of many shapes and colours. We might feel the breeze on our skin, smell salt in the air, hear sea gulls fighting over an abandoned french fry. With this subjective lens, we are better equipped to experience a multidimensional, multi-layered sense of the coastline. The more we look, the less defined the beach seems against the water. More details and more nuances emerge, and any rendering of the coastline seems less and less accurate.

At the beach, we can see that, far from being linear and static, a coastline is complex and emergent. It's constantly changing with the ebbs and flows of tides. It interacts with gravity and with the plants, animals, and micro-organisms that exist there. Not to mention, *our very presence* at the beach inevitably changes it in some ways, the pattern of waves shifting as water laps around our feet, our body's weight displacing sand.

And so, if we're checking in on how accurate or valid our perception is, it becomes more reasonable to say that *any* representation of a coastline—even the ways we represent it to ourselves through our direct perception—is never completely accurate. It can't be, since it's always in the process of becoming a new version of itself.

Our individual view of the shoreline is situated and contextual, shaped by where we stand, the coordinates in space (including how tall we are). Who we are matters in the act of knowing, although that's not a static equation either. We, too, are changed by the experience. At a beach, our eye colour might appear bluer. Our body's composition becomes more infused with molecules from the beach. We interact with the beach. We are part of the beach.

Our perception of anything can work this way, too. The point is, whether we're at a shoreline or getting intuitive hits, we're always, inextricably involved in the process of knowing. Perception is not something that merely happens *to* us. It happens within us. We have a role in creating our perceptions.

In the quantum sense, we could say that perception is intra-active. As Raymond Trevor Bradley writes, "The act of perception generates an outgoing wave field of attentional emotional energy directed to an object of interest that interacts with an incoming wave field of energy from the object."[26] The object and subject interact, creating a shift in both. (We know this as the observer effect, from the double slit experiment that demonstrated the wave-particle duality of light.)

In this explanation of nonlocal perception, the body-mind picks up on nonlocal information by entering into coherence with it. We resonate with—and as—the thing we perceive, and are changed by the experience of perceiving.

BOTH/AND, NONDUAL LOGIC

When we accept concepts like resonance and nonlocal connection, we make room to entertain a different way to understand what knowledge is—and even what truth is. And this can be really helpful when we want to understand intuition. Outdated assumptions about knowledge and validity lead us to think about the truth or correctness of intuition according to binary values: "Is this right or wrong for me?" But because of the nonlocal, nondual nature of intuition, the answer might be both! Rather than either, or, something might be right or good in some ways, and not in other respects. Both, and. For example, sometimes intuitive hits steer us towards growth, which can feel painful or awkward in the moment but is ultimately beneficial. In that case, the binary question of yes or no is too limiting.

Other times we perceive a whole intuitive vision but don't get information about what to do as a first step towards creating that vision. Expecting intuitive experience to proceed in a linear way probably causes us to discount so many valuable hits, simply because they're not appearing in the order we expect them to arrive—or in the form we would like.

As an uncertain and transpersonal process, intuition disrupts the binary of yes or no, is or is not. That's why it's important to refer to intuition as a process, a mode, or a way, rather than as a skill or a source. Intuition *happens*. As a dynamic relationship between the knower and the known, intuition thrives in a liminal space, somewhere in between. The process of knowing and the content of knowledge are not separate. As an expression of entanglement, where knowledge and the knower are not distinct, content and consciousness are entangled parts of a greater whole. We don't 'have' an intuition (or any knowledge); we interact with it, in a holistic, unfolding process. We enact and are enacted upon by knowing.

Whenever we say that something 'is,' we reinforce duality. Something either is or isn't. But with the lens of dimensionality, we know that reality varies in different contexts. Depending on where and how we're looking, there are different functional realities. For example, on the micro-level of particles smaller than atoms (protons, electrons, quarks, etc.) the laws of physics appear to work differently. In the quantum sense, quantum objects are waves. The theory is pretty clear on this point.[27] Until we observe them, they have "neither a unique location nor a unique state."[28] But when we measure those objects, we see that they are particles, situated in space and time. This wave-particle duality is usually interpreted as the wave and the particle existing at the same time, but more accurately, the wave-form exists *outside* of time.[29]

In our 'normal' functional reality, a table looks really solid. Definitely solid enough to be painful when we stub our toe on it in the middle of the night. But we also know that table (as with every solid, material object) is comprised primarily of space; of energy. Both are right. Newtonian physics, the framework that has supported our understanding of the physical universe, still holds up. *And* the quantum physics that blow Newton's framing out of the water also work. Both, and. (They work on different scales of experience, in different domains.)

Identity works the same way. In the rational era, with our binary assumptions, we tend to frame ourselves as self-contained and independent. And to some extent, this is true, especially when we gaze out into the world and see things that aren't us. But the separate, separated version of ourselves is only one way to understand our existence. In a quantum framing, the notion of the bounded singularity of a person or a psyche is not the whole picture. While it is true that I am not the tree I see while looking out my window, we both exist within the same field that enfolds us and generates form. We (the tree and I) are connected (and can even—in some states of mind—communicate).[30]

So, in this sense, self and other are not a binary pair—they're not even really separate at all.

We don't even have to reach into ideas about the quantum field to see our interconnectedness. In very material ways, we all depend on each other for existence, for our very survival. We're not bounded singular identities at all; we are intra-connected assemblages, systems within systems within systems. But nonduality is helpful in explaining some experiences of intuition—experiences of energy awareness, empathic resonance, and psychic experience. In the unseen dimension, where I am not separate from you, our minds can be known to each other (telepathy). I am not separate from, say, a chair or that tree outside my window, and in moments of clear access to the undifferentiated awareness (field of consciousness) that we both simultaneously encompass and belong to, I can know if the chair is about to break or the tree is about to get struck by lightning (precognition).

The nondual, akashic logic that helps us understand intuition disrupts a binary sense of right and wrong (correct and incorrect) because more than one thing can be true at the same time. Yet even when we can recognize this nuance intellectually, our habits tend to draw us into one or the other. We're so used to either/or. The binary is so embedded it seems truthful. But by working to develop a habit of both/and, we can come to realize that, even if we don't always experience it this way, things can be separate and discrete in certain dimensions *and* be inherently entangled in others.

TRUTH

By reckoning with intuition on its own terms, we create an opportunity to deepen our frame of reference for what counts as real and valid when it comes to…well, everything, including our experiences of conscious awareness. A quantum, intuitive framework lets us extend what counts as truth beyond scientific materialism, and helps us consider ideas and concepts that stretch our imagination of the nature of reality.

Here's how that works: In the space-time paradigm, if we can't tell whether something is true or untrue, the presumption is that we just don't have enough knowledge about the thing. There's an underlying belief that if we don't know something, it's because we just don't know it *yet*.

But outside of space-time, in the realm of potential, we accept that knowing might never come. The quantum field is inherently uncertain, and something existing in a state of potential doesn't mean it will actualize. Even the location of electrons is understood to exist within a field or cloud of probability. The best we can know is the probable location. That's why it's possible to intuit things that don't end up coming into being: we have captured knowledge of a potential.

Within a quantum logic, we have to accept that there are some things we can't know in that same sense of knowing, but we still know them. We recognize this with intuition because intuition lets us know things we don't know how to put into language. Not being distinct or concrete doesn't mean something can't be true. Remember intuition's non-discursive character. It's possible to know things that are difficult or even impossible to put into words.

Here we bump up against the inconvenient constraints of the English language. Other languages inherently recognize different orders of knowing. There's knowing in the sense of connecting, or relating, and there's knowing in the sense of "I have knowledge of." In any language, the scientific approach tends to equate naming a thing with knowing it. It's almost like a form of ownership. But just because you know what to call something doesn't mean you know what it really is. Herbalist and philosopher Stephen Harrod Buhner makes the point that naming actually *interferes* with intuitive knowing.[31]

And even though I've argued against the imperative to know everything through the scientific lens, much of the quantum framework I'm talking about here has been, and will continue to be, demonstrated scientifically as time goes on. These things just take a long time sometimes. For example, a tiny material condensate first proposed in 1924 by Bose and Einstein was finally demonstrated in 1995. It took seven decades for the instruments that could do this to be developed![32] We used to believe that laws of nature remain fixed under every circumstance, but these so-called laws have turned out to be not quite as fixed as we thought. Even the constant speed of light has been updated[33]—more than once—due to refinement in measurement technology. Not to mention, the speed of light is not the absolute speed limit we had thought. Experiments with entanglement and bi-location show us that information can and does move faster than light.

So how do we recognize validity and correctness within an unfolding, emergent context? How do we know what's true? When it comes to intuition, we can focus on the experience of being, in the moment. Intuitive logic is not necessarily causal. It works with correlation, correspondence, synchrony, and other ways of making sense, and we can become more alive to those dynamics of resonance. We can recognize the complexity of connections and interconnections that comprise intuitive experience. We can trust that we don't have all the information (yet) and focus on the next right step.

Quantum themes show us choices in the ways we can interact with intuitive experience. With a logic of indeterminacy, we can recognize there's something there—some information, some energy, some connection to be made—even if we don't know what it is yet. We can become increasingly aware of our interconnectedness beyond the boundaries of time and space we're used to experiencing. And we can learn to trust that an intuitive hit is informational, even if it doesn't reveal details or a definitive confidence. The logic shows us that there might not be one definitive answer. There are only answers, decisions to be made, and consequences. There are only forks in the road.

A MODE OF RESONANCE & CONNECTION

The quantum-akashic paradigm points us to a way of conceptualizing how a person can connect—intuitively—with knowledge across, through, and beyond the dimensions of space and/or time. Information, in the form of energy, exists encoded on waves in a distributed pattern, kind of like a hologram. Intuition works by resonance, and by our consciousness connecting with vibrational content we're not usually aware of. When we resonate to the vibration of a thing, we're intuiting or 'grabbing' from the akashic dimension. Then, when we're being receptive, in flow, this content can become more accessible to our individual minds.

Intuition then is a way of experiencing transpersonal, or collective, aspects of life—a (multi-dimensional) context that we're connected to because we're also embedded in it. This context is the foundation of consciousness, the realm in which we dream, find visions, hear voices, and participate in all manner of non-ordinary experience. On the level of consciousness, we are even more intricately connected than we realize—to the transpersonal repository of archetypes, myths, and symbols known as the collective unconscious *and* to the thoughts, feelings, and desires of other beings. And we remain connected to this dimension of consciousness as part of our make-up, even if we often forget the parts of ourselves that aren't merely contained in the physical form.

With this in mind, one possible way to explain intuitive experience is that it relies on porous boundaries between our conscious awareness and our collective unconscious. We've only lost our 'sense' of oneness, not the reality of it. Our oneness remains true; it's just in a dimension of experience we generally don't perceive (or tend to ignore). That means cultivating intuition involves allowing more of what exists into our subjective awareness.

Within a rational, linear, binary construction of knowledge, subjectivity is a liability. But with intuitive experience, the subject's interaction with the information/knowledge/awareness is vital.

This becomes a counter-cultural stance to take, because we're used to truth being achieved objectively—where the knower doesn't (or can't) matter.

Trusting intuition on its own terms means choosing a framework for thinking about consciousness and connection that values human experience as a complex, holistic, subjective process and that recognizes (metaphorically) that we are at a shoreline of our own inner experience—a dynamic participant in our perception.

With this framing, intuition is a function of connection: to ourselves, to each other, to our situation (situatedness), to the cosmos, to our ancestors, to our descendants, to the elements, to the archetypes. Intuition demonstrates our intimate connection with all that is—all that exists now, and all that has ever been and will be.

Intuition acts as a mode of connection between parts of ourselves we don't always have access to (or don't realize we do) because it's all us anyway. The experience of non-ordinary states of mind enables us to feel connected to a collective unity that's composed of more dimensions than we can see or sense with any of our ordinary, outward senses. This resonance can give rise to a sense of coherence and meaning. And honestly, it's no wonder we often attribute this knowing to a source outside of ourselves. It's that big. It's that amazing. But it's time to claim this as a feature and ability of human consciousness—we just have to recognize the dynamic, complex, holistic fact of existence.

Is the new paradigm correct? Laszlo says, eh, we don't know.[34] But it's the best we can do right now. The intellectual territory we have to inhabit to let intuition stand on its own terms might not be logical, objective, or even scientifically valid in ways we're used to. So far, we don't have a definitive answer about how intuition works, and that's okay, because intuitive experience relies on the unique configuration of the intuiting person. Experience is subjective, and the entirety of our experience and context shapes how we perceive, know, and understand.

Plus, as quantum theory tells us, things can only be certain in the abstract (or, in other words, in a dimension of potential). We can speculate and make best guesses and even be quite sure about how true something is using calculations, but in the intuitive moment, what matters is your cultivated trust in the experience, regardless of how energetic sensitivity, precognition, or any other intuitive experience works. Once we're talking about actual things in the actual world, how they manifest becomes much less certain.

Simply put, scientific certainty is only one kind of truth. Since intuitive experience is often without language, and since each of us has different ways of registering what's taking place for us in the unseen dimensions, intuition on its own terms requires that we stretch our personal understanding of what it means to know.

Chapter 4

A PRAXIS FOR CULTIVATING INTUITION

Each of us has the capacity for intuitive experience. All of us can cultivate a personal relationship with our intuitive function.

And while we're all intuitive, it also seems that some people are more intuitive than others. This isn't a judgment. Just a fact. Like how some people are more emotionally intelligent or more rational or better at math. For some people, intuition is such a natural, easy way of being that they aren't even aware of it as they use it. And for others of us, accessing and trusting intuition is not so easy-breezy. We might understand that intuition is a valuable companion of consciousness, but we're not in the regular habit of hearing it or recognizing what it has to say.

Recognizing our intuitive capabilities can be complicated because we all use and connect to intuitive experience differently. There are such diverse types of content that we can come to know, and the intuitive mode shows up for each of us in unique ways. Some people are intuitive in the sense that they can connect deeply to other people's emotional vibes. Others are best at knowing their own next right move. Still others can intuitively sense the influx of collective waves, trends, or events. Some intuitive experiences are practical, while others don't seem to have a function. For example, I often have an intuitive sense of the big picture—a visionary sense of the future. I remember being about seven years old in the 1980s, struck by the intuitive impression of a scene where people could communicate with each other by a computer-like device worn on their wrists, like a watch. I might have been on to something, but that kind of prophetic inner vision doesn't necessarily help me decide whether I should book my dentist appointment for this Tuesday or next.

Most importantly, no matter where any of us start on the intuitive spectrum, *we can all cultivate our intuitive abilities*. Remember

Estés's story of Vasalisa, whose doll gets carried around in her pocket? She needs to be fed. We have to nurture our intuition. And we can do this by following a path of intentional practice.

The path of practice for cultivating intuition arises from understanding intuition on its own terms. Everything we know intuition to be—all of it, from sudden realizations to experiences of transpersonal awareness—shapes *how* we go about developing a relationship to intuitive experience. And while I told you in chapter 1 that this will be more of a *why-to* book than a *how-to*, this second half of the book explores the why of intuition development—the why of the how, if you will.

In the first half of the book, I've laid out a theory about intuition on its own terms. Here's a quick summary of what we've learned so far:

- Intuition is an experience, process, or way of knowing (or mode of consciousness).
- Experiencing intuition is a relationship; a matter of connection and resonance.

Now, we add a third tenet. While understanding intuition on its own terms can help us accept and enhance intuitive experiences, a framework of any kind doesn't cultivate intuitive experience on its own. *Practice* does.

This path of practice can help improve anyone's intuition, no matter how intuitive (or not) you think you are. Intuition development is a process anchored in self-awareness and self-compassion, that helps us connect more deeply with our consciousness and context (inner and outer experience). If there's an underlying belief to this book, it's that pursuing intuition development enhances our relationship to ourselves and encourages us to live more fully, with more ease and connection.

What follows in this part of the book is a discussion of resources and strategies for cultivating an intuitive way of being in the world.[i]

PRACTICE AS PRACTICE

Before I say even one word about the components of intuition development, I want to address what seems to be an epidemic of anxiety about self-development and self-improvement. For those of us raised in the neo-liberal, consumer-capitalist culture, there is a widespread feeling that we should always be bettering ourselves, that we must continuously work to become better than we are. Self-cultivation as self-care and as community-care gets interpreted as self-improvement, usually for the benefit of material (not psycho-spiritual) goals. I can only hope that thinking about cultivating intuition does not add to anyone's anxiety or feelings of inadequacy. I'm not suggesting that someone *should* pursue this path of self-development—only that it is possible. It's here if you want it.

You don't actually have to *do* anything to be more intuitive, other than realize that you are already intuitive. But, if you do want to trust your intuition more, and have it be more present for you, that's possible, too. We practice intuition development so intuitive perception can become second nature, so that it arises more readily and so we are receptive and alert to intuitive experiences when they arise. With practice, we can come to trust our intuitive experiences because we have developed the ability to discern the meanings contained in our unique intuitive expression.

---

[i] For even more suggestions and encouragement around the inner work of cultivating your intuition, see the resources available at www.WhatisIntuition.ca

Over time, practice lets us recognize the feeling of intuitive experience for what it is—intuition—as opposed to fear, desire, or projection. Through practice, we learn to discern the different communicative channels that exist in our psyche. Through the gut, where we can recognize butterflies and excitement as distinct from indigestion; goosebumps and flushes on the skin; smells, visual disturbances, inner visions and experiences from any of the other senses; and signals from the mind, its thought processes, and habits of attention. Over time, we get in touch with what it feels like to hear the small, still, inner voice that guides us away from harm and towards wholeness.

And while I can tell you about these techniques and even guide you through how to do them, without you putting in the (inner) work, nothing much will happen.

The most important takeaway here is that this path of practice is an ongoing process, not a project. Intuitive development is never perfected. This is because the techniques for cultivating intuition are transformative. As we undertake them, we are changed and our experiences change. And since we are always changing and developing and there is always more 'self' to unpack, there is no ultimate arrival point or mastery, though there can be more ease. (And please don't think of this as a call to struggle or to endlessly seek more achievement. It's just a note that practice is a lifelong process of unfolding awareness. Remember: We are fine. We don't need fixing.)

CULTIVATING INTUITION IS TRANSFORMATIVE PRAXIS

The process of becoming more attuned to intuitive experience gets variously called awakening, discovering, uncovering, igniting, and more; words that describe a process of realization. They all point to the idea that the capacity to be intuitive is already present but that it has been covered up, hidden, or forgotten beneath layers of culture, values, and assumptions.

And if intuition is a capacity, then cultivating it involves more than mastering techniques. It's not just something we learn to do. It's someone we become. Through practice we *become* more self-aware, more receptive to intuitive experience, and more able to intelligently discern its meaning.

The practices re-orient our attention and awareness, creating an enhanced relationship to our lives that becomes the foundation of intuitive experience. The result is living more fully; being more present, more connected, more engaged. As we come to experience, who we are (and who we might become) and what we know (what we *can* know) are not distinct factors.

The contemplative and reflective work of intuition development connects us more directly with the context of our experience. We come to know ourselves as we are in the present and recognize who we are in relation to the context of our lives. Then, as we shift how we relate to our inner and outer experiences, we can come to know more. Along the way, we might need to unpack aspects of ourselves we have neatly tucked away, and restore wholeness to our psyche. This is healing work.

The program of practice for cultivating intuition laid out here can help us transform—even revolutionize—how we relate to commonly held assumptions about all kinds of things: what can be known, *who* can know, who we even *are*. Doing this work actually expands our context into dimensions of conscious experience beyond what we previously knew to be available. And in this way, becoming more intuitive also means coming into greater awareness of aspects of our world that many don't even consider as real. Yes, the multidimensional invisible world; the unseen.

As a result of these practices, our self-identity might shift. We may start to identify more strongly with aspects of the self beyond the surface and outside the individual ego, like the personal unconscious and collective, intersubjective consciousness. We might move from thinking of ourselves as a solitary, conscious individual to knowing ourselves as an interdependent, multidimensional being. Shifting how we identify, we can move into increased resonance with psychic vibrations and begin to perceive, recognize, and act on intuitive impressions.

The techniques presented here are developmental practices that belong to transpersonal psychology and, more importantly, to the wisdom traditions and schools of philosophy that have engaged in these psychological, philosophical, and spiritual activities for thousands of years, seeking 'moreness' to enrich and enable a deeper, more ethical, and more meaningful life. What they have in common are they're all undertaken to enable transformation, a "deliberate change in consciousness."[35]

And that's why I'm calling intuition development a *praxis*. **Praxis** refers to embodying or practicing ideas and values. More than learning about ideas, there's a commitment to living those ideas out in the world. There's an implication that the practice is done with a commitment to acting in ways that serve to heal the world and change society for the better. The educator Paulo Freire defined praxis as "reflection and action upon the world in order to transform it."[36] This echoes an idea embedded in New Age culture: That psycho-spiritual transformation and the practices that we do to cultivate it don't only change the individuals who undertake them, but that this work can also bring about societal change.

We're not only changing ourselves by doing this work—we're changing the world. (I told you this was healing work!)

INTRODUCING INTUITIVE LIFE PRACTICE

The path of practice for cultivating intuition rests on three interconnected pillars: mindset, awareness, and discernment.

By 'mindset' I mean a mind that is prepared with knowing what intuition is. The practice in this pillar is cultivating an orientation to valuing intuitive experience, even when it's uncanny or weird and violates taboos. The 'awareness' pillar refers to a body and mind that is prepared to pay attention to intuitive experience. It's all about cultivating a relaxed, receptive consciousness; calm attention, nuanced sensitivity, receptive awareness, being in flow, and creative or restful surrender. And 'discernment' is the ability to understand or to judge wisely. Here, we cultivate a willingness to be uncertain and bear the 'risk' of that uncertainty, in balance with a nuanced sense of conviction. Discernment is a habit of self-awareness that helps us learn to trust our intuitive experiences and to recognize ourselves as trustworthy, intuitive beings.

Each of these pillars of practice is important, but remember: this is a why-to book, not a how-to. Everyone doesn't need to do all the practices. As transformative praxis, intuitive life practice is a matter of strengthening and deepening your relationship with yourself. Rather than it being a program, think of cultivating intuition as a direction of development; a lifelong journey to becoming more intuitive—and in the process, of becoming more of who you are.

Chapter 5
PILLAR 1: MINDSET

In the first pillar of practice, we cultivate a mindset that is conducive to trustworthy intuitive experience. As we've explored, there are so many different ways to conceive of intuition: what it is, where it comes from, and how it works. Intuitive experience is complex! The reason this matters is because what you believe about intuition informs how you relate to it. So, before we get to the *skills* of intuition development—the skills of perceiving and interpreting intuitive experience—we lay a foundation of mindset.

In this pillar, we unpack our beliefs in—and our stories about—intuition. We dig into why intuition is still subject to taboos and misunderstanding. We look into elements that cause us to reject and shut down intuitive experience in ourselves, and consider how certain beliefs and ideas act as a cloudy filter that disengages us from being in the intuitive mode, and prevents us from even recognizing intuitive experiences when they happen.

One reason shifting your mindset matters so much is that, with an orientation to valuing intuitive experience, you simply start to recognize it happening more often. Typically, attunement to subtle and inner experience is driven by a willingness to experience these things. Even just recognizing the possibility of intuitive experience prepares a person to experience more of it. In other words, when we intentionally align ourselves with the possibility of intuitive function, our access to intuition tends to improve. So, to become more intuitive, we have to believe that intuition is both possible and valuable.

Mindset primes our receptivity. We prepare our expectations deliberately so that, over time, we're more likely to receive more intuitive information. Simply believing or trusting that you can have valuable intuitive experiences goes a long way towards improving your intuition—even if you do nothing else. By letting yourself entertain the idea that you might perceive intuitive information at any time, a recursive, positive feedback loop develops. By expecting it, you make the experience more likely. Then, if we pay attention and act on intuitive hits, our relationship with intuition gets even better.

This feedback loop is fuelled by trust and self-awareness.

So this is the first pillar for cultivating intuition: developing a mindset comprised of a willingness to accept that all kinds of intuitive experience is available, and a curiosity about how it shows up for you. By thinking about the framework that lets intuition make sense on its own terms, you are engaging in mindset practice. And look at that. By reading this book, your mindset practice has already begun.

METAPHYSICAL CHOICES

Mindset is a buzzy word. Generally, it means our attitudes and orientations towards a topic. Mindset is our way of thinking, our beliefs, and our ideas, and it's connected to cognition, attitudes, values and frame of mind. Mindset is similar to **worldview**, a fundamental set of beliefs, values, assumptions, and ideas about the world. Most often, mindsets are unconscious. They're internalized, so they remain hidden, even from ourselves.

But our thoughts and minds' habits can change, which is pretty noteworthy because we *need* our minds on board when we want to become better attuned to intuitive experience.

Whether we're aware of it or not (usually not), in every moment we make metaphysical choices. These are assumptions we make about the world and the nature of reality that in turn structure what we think of as real (and even of what is possible). Metaphysical choices are beliefs we take for granted, and though they're usually not conscious, they frame what we think of as real, normal, and good.[37]

So, this pillar has implications beyond intuition and intuitive experience. As we examine what we believe about intuition, we also explore what we believe about ourselves, who we are and what we're doing here, incarnate and alive on earth. We explore the nature of truth, and reality, and consciousness. Big questions, right?

And although I say metaphysical *choice*, it's not like we can just tell ourselves to believe otherwise and that's that. It can be incredibly difficult to parse out alternatives to the ways of knowing and being that we grew up with. We have to work to change our feelings about our beliefs. We have to work to embody them. We have to re-pattern how we relate to reality.

But why do we even need to develop a particular mindset about intuition? If intuition is a birthright, connected to instinct and something we are born with already, shouldn't it be easy or obvious? Let's start there.

A couple summers back, I met a neighbour and we got to chatting. She asked what I 'do' and I told her that I study and write about intuition, what it is, and why that matters.

Well. She had such an interesting response. Her body kind of stiffened; she stood up straighter as she told me (repeatedly, defensively, I could practically see the hackles) that she believes in—heck, is all for—gut feelings. But. She draws a line at intuition. In a tone I recognized from some of my former academic colleagues, she adamantly demanded that I hear her on this point: "There's no such thing! It's not possible!" (She meant psychic intuition and energetic sensitivity.)

And you know what? For her, she might be right. She might live her whole life and never experience transpersonal intuition. Even if it came in like a storm and dropped a golf-ball-sized chunk of hail on her head, she would probably have all kinds of rationalizations for it, rather than acknowledge intuitive experience.

Now, you'll notice that my neighbour was okay with gut feelings. She was willing to allow for the existence of intuition as long as there was a material, rational explanation. That's fine if it works for her, but it's unfortunate, because as we know, limiting what counts as intuition to whatever can be explained rationally creates a shallow, simplistic understanding of how it works.

Ultimately, rational explanations don't account for intuition on its own terms. They exclude intuitive experiences not based on prior experience or another recognizable source, which many of the common (yet admittedly uncanny) experiences are not—experiences like suddenly realizing you should probably take a different route home today or getting a call from a long-lost friend you've just been thinking about. Something is lost by not recognizing that intuition is a relationship that we can have with ourselves and with information carried along vibrations that we somehow perceive and interpret to make sense of. It denies a whole range of psychic and transpersonal experience.

Mindset matters because, piled on top of innate intuitive knowing, there are layers of cultural conditioning that teach us over and over again how impossible it is that we can know. We're taught that only certain authorities have the right to know—teachers, priests, parents—and while, yes, there are things experts know better than us, that's not everything. There's the matter of being able to trust what we know ourselves, from within, through the connection each of us have with our own innate wisdom, and with transpersonal consciousness. It's about being experts in our own experience and coming at that from a critical, educated lens (meaning we are educated in our own 'stuff' and critical of the ways our 'stuff' is constructed by outside forces). There's the need to be willing to see our context with receptive curiosity rather than preconceived notions.

Perhaps most importantly, mindset matters because it shapes the way our consciousness filters our thoughts and experiences. When we actively acknowledge the possibility for intuitive experience, we are much more likely to experience that possibility.

Because to some extent, whether we register intuitive hits at all depends on what we think they are. For example, if you have a tingling sensation in your gut, do you know that's how your intuition communicates? Or do you just chalk it up to indigestion? When we actively acknowledge the possibility for intuitive experience, we are much more likely to recognize that possibility.

I was talking to my aunt about my research one day, and describing different kinds of intuitive experience. When I got to synchronicity—"you know, where you think of someone out of the blue, and then a while later you take a different-than-usual route home and there that person is"—her eyes lit up with recognition. "Oh yeah, I know that," she said, remembering a time when that exact thing happened to her. "I guess I didn't know that's a thing."

She had had that experience, but had no way to categorize what it was. So she forgot about it...until our conversation.

In 2001, more than half of the U.S. population reported having psychic experiences.[38] That's a lot of people. So why the heck do I still encounter deniers? Maybe you're one of them? Or maybe you're not outright denying the possibility of intuitive experiences but you're skeptical. Herein lies the work of the mindset pillar. Without this preparatory practice, we might not recognize intuition when it arises—or we might dismiss psychic awareness as something else entirely. Unless we're prepared to consider that psychic intuitive experiences are real and possible, we might overlook them, even as they're happening.

Mindset isn't simply just about whether intuition exists or not. Since what we believe about intuition informs how (and even if) we experience it, we'd best wade through our ideas to figure out what we believe about intuition. Without a guiding framework or a notion of its source, it's easy to project whatever you believe into what intuition is and where it's from.

Importantly here, what we believe about intuition informs what we do to help cultivate it. For example, if we believe intuition to be the voices of guides or angels (of the biblical or library variety), we will want to deepen our relationship to those beings. If we believe intuition is made possible by expertise, then we'd go about gaining expertise. Or, if you agree with me that intuition is a function of resonance and connection facilitated by a receptive and self-aware consciousness, you would take up the path of practice I'm outlining here.

The mindset for cultivating intuition concerns how we understand ourselves as conscious beings in relation to consciousness itself. In Chapter 3, we explored how intuition makes sense on its own terms, within a quantum logic of resonance and connection. If intuitive experience works in the ways I've suggested, what does that mean for our understanding of ourselves? Or for the way consciousness works in general?

For example, some people say that intuition arises from a subconscious aspect of the psyche, so how we conceptualize the psyche matters to how we relate to intuition.

We all carry inherited beliefs about the self and the psyche. From the beginnings of the psychoanalytic traditions of the 19th century, the psyche has been portrayed as a dark, foreboding place that we don't really *want* to know too much about. It's scary! We don't tend to bother with it unless it bothers us, at which point we might seek out a psychoanalyst or psychiatrist to help us uncover whatever is misaligned or unwell about this part of ourselves. In general, when we hear too much from the subconscious, we tend to pathologize these experiences rather than treat them as opportunities for self-awareness and growth. That's a mindset that might lead us to pathologize intuitive experience too, framing it as freaky, alarming, or even unwelcome—rather than as a resource for potential wisdom and understanding. And with the feedback loop intuition relies on for affirmation, this internalized attitude communicates to the intuitive function that it should retreat. We have made it clear that it is not welcome, and often, the result is it leaves us alone.

See why intuition makes people like my neighbour so damn defensive?

WHERE KNOWLEDGE COMES FROM

Within the mindset pillar, we check in with our beliefs about consciousness, knowledge and about truth itself. To let intuition make sense, we need to consider: What counts as knowledge? How do we come to know something? These are deep, philosophical orientations that lay the groundwork for how we relate to intuition in general—and to our own intuitive experience.

So much of intuitive experience—things like pre-cognition and telepathy—have for so long been considered literally impossible, according to a knowledge framework that only trusts objective, material rationality as the valid way to know anything. Throw in a longstanding taboo against intuition and the unseen world, and it can feel like human nature to cast doubt first instead of trust. After all, doubt is a foundation of the scientific paradigm and of the analytic mode.

And this goes beyond the issue of trusting ourselves. (Of course it does!) Because another foundation of the rational approach is that knowledge must be objective. But objectivity requires us to hold our subjectivity at bay, meaning we can never be fully invested or immersed in anything. Over time, this effort can cause anxiety and stress that interfere with the receptivity required of intuition. (Because intuition thrives with a mindset of trust—not doubt.)

Starting from a default of doubt and objectivity prevents us from being present to the moment, leading to a state of alienation. I use the word 'alienation' deliberately here, to remind us that this disconnection from intuitive experience is not a personal failing but a result of internalized socialization and cultural factors. Our whole collective way of being disavows intuitive knowing, constrained by barriers that the capitalist-materialist mindset has constructed against knowing what we are experiencing. When we don't recognize ourselves to be part of the web of life, our relationship with intuition suffers. We become estranged from our own bodies and emotions and from an appreciation for the sentience that exists beyond the human species.

While some of the internalized doubt and skepticism may be well-founded and even useful, much of it is excessive, having become habit. And habits, as we know, become unconscious, reliant on well-worn neural pathways rather than intention.

So how do we respond to inner knowing, through this veil of disconnection and deadening of the world?

How can we understand ourselves and the world beyond the lens of dualist (me/not me, inner/outer, good/bad) and finite (scarcity of time, space, knowledge, potential) values? Well, we unpack the foundations that inform our way of thinking about intuition.

Through the mindset pillar, we practice cultivating a more expansive worldview. By becoming aware of the boundaries of our perception (and hence, the limitations of our knowledge), we grow beyond, or transcend, them. Doing inner work that helps us recognize our beliefs and assumptions about what intuition is prepares us for a different way of seeing and sensing. Through the work of the mindset pillar, we shift our orientation to intuitive experience, helping us become more comfortable, familiar, and confident. Rather than shut down possibility and potential, this opens a door to opportunity for making different metaphysical choices.

OVERCOMING TWO MISGUIDED PARADIGMS

A mindset that is prepared to cultivate intuition on its own terms requires that we learn to see beyond the lens of our inherited values, taboos, and assumptions about consciousness, knowledge, and intuition.

Those assumptions tend to follow one of two common themes. In one, intuition is positioned as perfectly reasonable and explainable in rational, materialist terms (like my neighbour's comfortable gut feeling or the academic favourite, expertise). I call this *misconception*, the problem of misunderstanding intuition *as if* it's rational or cognitive. On the other end of the spectrum is *mystification*, where intuition gets set up as inherently magical, divine, and transcendent; a connection that only some special people have access to. *Mystification* makes intuitive experiences inaccessible by creating unrealistic expectations of what intuition is supposed to look and feel like.

These two misguided paradigms each stem from beliefs, or metaphysical choices that are embedded in differing cultural frameworks. For example, I've already referred to the wisdom traditions in the Hindu-Buddhist lineages, where intuitive knowing is received as a matter of course. In the European lineage, we can trace our assumptions about knowledge through the Romantic era, towards the end of the 18th century, when folks were invested in, and committed to, experiences that were explicitly *not* rational, logical, or analytic. Poets like Blake and Wordsworth underscored the value of mystical, animist, and intuitive experience. Wordsworth described intuition as "authentic tidings of invisible things," while Blake wrote, "If the doors of perception were cleansed everything would appear as it is, infinite." The Romantics *glorified* intuition for its direct access to knowledge. They were all for it.

But after the Romantic period, in a kind of backlash, the modern Enlightenment era locked on to the idea that development—aka scientific progress—was the foremost value. Enlightenment thinkers like Locke and Descartes exemplified the de-contextualization of this era, working to rid European philosophy of frameworks that evoked superstition, and maligning the changeability of emotion as untrustworthy. Analysis and objectivity became the preferred, acceptable way to understand our reality. Embodiment and connection with nature became a liability, thought to reflect inferior or primitive consciousness rather than being a relational, meaningful way of accessing knowledge. And of course, this movement rejected intuition as a way of knowing, equating it with unscientific, unproven ideas and ideals.

In 2022, when I'm writing this, these two divergent approaches to knowledge production are still in play. One of these, the rational-intellectual-analytical mode, is familiar as the primary mode of European Enlightenment reasoning. It favours rational analysis and skews towards reductionism, a process of trying to understand complex systems by reducing them to their component parts. It focuses on objectively measurable factors and on data obtainable by the scientific method. Based in a belief that the world is essentially fixed, it presumes that when something is true, it is true universally and objectively. This framework abides by the assumption that knowledge is separate from the knower, so it looks for truth in external reality.[39] The primary metaphor that informs this mode is the machine, as it imagines the workings of nature as essentially mechanical.[40]

The second approach, the "holistic-intuitive-depth"[41] mode, has been the primary way our species has made sense of the world for most of its history, and it's still dominant throughout indigenous cultures. It perceives the wholes of things; valuing systems and complexity, recognizing that reality is situational, complex, and dynamic; and it doesn't require language or labelling for something to pass as 'known'. This holistic-intuitive mode recognizes that knowledge—and especially what we know through dreams and revelation—is not separable from the knower, so it includes both the knower and their lived context[i] as integral aspects of an ongoing, unfolding relationship of knowledge production. This mode is more likely to see the world through a metaphor of flow—think a garden or a dance—or through a quantum-akashic metaphor that recognizes multidimensionality and nondual entanglement.

These two modes of knowing are obviously quite different from each other. They *feel* different and often produce knowledge in different domains. It can be tempting to want to rank them, which is a common methodology in the hierarchy-loving rational-analytic framework, but really, they are complementary.

Unpacking these two distinct modes (the rational-analytic-materialist mode and the intuitive-holistic-depth mode) has helped me understand why some people are so reluctant to recognize the psychic aspects of intuition, and why others insist that intuitive content is always, absolutely perfect, with divine origin.

Using the framework of these two modes of knowing also sheds light on why we might be disconnected from, or mistrusting of,

---

i When I say "the lived context," I mean *everything* a person experiences and has experienced. Everything they breathe, eat, love, create, and desire; the built environment; and the dynamic relationships that inform habits, behaviour, and experience.

intuitive experience. It explains the conflict many of us experience around our own intuitive experience, like the presence of an inner critic who pre-emptively rejects what we intuitively know to be true because it doesn't make sense according to how we think it *should* be. Or the theorists who still point to fast cognition and say, 'Only rational stuff going on here!' The rational-analytic mode doesn't let intuition make sense on its own terms. And within a materialist paradigm that dismisses psychic intuition as mystical, as woo-woo, or as non-ordinary, *any* of our lived experiences are at risk of being dismissed as insignificant or non-existent, especially if they are uncanny, mysterious or otherwise unexplainable.

MISCONCEPTION OF INTUITION

Most of us raised and educated within a cognitive, analytically-biased culture have internalized a superiority complex about rationality. As a result, we tend to feel judge-y about the likelihood that the intuitive mode can provide reliable, useful knowledge. These beliefs operate behind the scenes, telling us that analysis is a more advanced way to process information, that it is better and more sophisticated, that it reflects advancement from the more primitive intuitive processing. This story we tell ourselves (our mindset) about knowledge makes it seem that not only are feelings not required in the act of knowing, but that feelings—or any of the non-rational functions—interfere with knowing. In this paradigm, only rational cognition can be counted as trustworthy. So, instead of meeting psychic experience with curiosity, we demand proof of its very existence, let alone its accuracy. We dismiss its value, labelling it as illogical or irrational.

The **hegemony** at work behind and underneath our knowledge systems makes it seem like analysis is the best, and in some cases the only, respectable mode for understanding the world and our role in it. The modern rational culture is so invested in the scientific-analytic paradigm that it doesn't recognize that analysis, science, and logic are only one way among others to produce knowledge. We tend to assume that what we can know through the rational-analytic mode is *all* there is to know.

And so misconception is one of the two mistakes or mis-characterizations that occur when we try to make sense of intuition according to a rational-analytic mindset. To make intuition fit into a rational-binary-materialist framework requires that we exclude any versions of intuitive experience (psychic experience, empathic resonance, etc.) that don't fit into that framework, and double down on the notion that intuition is reasonable, rational, and *definitely not transpersonal.*

That's why intuition-as-expertise has become the go-to explanation for a lot of experts, including psychologists.[ii] It sits comfortably within a framework that centres cognition and that prefers a linear model of causation over a holistic, interconnected frame of reference. It doesn't take any work to make this explanation align squarely with a rational-analytic lens. No stretch is required to understand how or what is happening. Intuition is simply a function of the brain; normal thinking that happens below the threshold of awareness.

---

ii   A recent *Psychology Today* article even described intuition as understood widely to be "nothing more than pattern recognition."

Limiting and constraining the idea of intuition to a definition that can be justified in rational terms is a mindset problem created by a dogmatic belief in the truth of rational, materialist science, also known as **scientism**. Let's take a brief dive into this important piece of mindset.

The scientific method (which involves testing hypotheses against empirical evidence and refining knowledge through iterations of experiments) is based on empirical evidence (meaning it comes from sensory experience), and phenomena get interpreted within the consensual laws of nature. Following the scientific method and using the principles of objectivity and triangulation, we presume that something is real or true if I can see, touch, or feel it *and* if another person can see, touch, or feel it; *and* if I can see, touch, or feel it again later, under replicated circumstances. All good, so far.

But there is an important difference between science—the *method* of discovery that favours inquiry, experimentation, and critical awareness—and **scientism**, a set of *beliefs* about the nature of truth and a commitment to science that transcends method. As a belief system, scientism enlists science as the only respectable way to know something. It establishes a mindset where knowledge is only valid to the extent that it adheres to the scientific method, instead of treating the rational-intellectual-analytic mode as a useful tool among others.

We have confused the *tool* of scientific method with the *philosophy* of scientism.[iii]

Scientism adheres to a number of dogmas, functioning almost like a religion.[iv] According to its tenets, science can tell us

---

[iii] This idea is borrowed from Charles T. Tart.
[iv] For more about the dogmas of scientism, I recommend Rupert Sheldrake's *The Science Delusion* (2012).

everything we need to know. Conversely, if something does not conform to scientific standards, well, we can't recognize it as true. Scientism reifies[v] doubt, linear development, and materialism; it values what can be seen (as opposed to what's unseen). It assumes that if we can't see or share what we feel we know, it can't possibly be real. For something to be considered true, the results must be triangulated. Knowledge must be measurable, achieved only through a formal, replicable methodology, and is only reliably procured through the practice of objective science, where an observer merely observes and does not (and indeed must not) interact with that which they are observing.

This framework generally assumes that if something is true, then it is true universally,[vi] meaning once knowledge is established, it remains true no matter who is looking. In the scientific process, the scientist (or whoever is working to know the thing) must remove themselves from the process of knowing. Then, we can trust that the knowledge is valid. But scientism goes further. Interpretation and subjectivity are worse than irrelevant; they pollute the ability to rely on such knowledge. In order to be trustworthy, subjectivity and specificity must be eliminated. Knowledge then becomes inert (static, unchanging) and objectified (decontextualized), removed from the dynamic relationship between the knower and what they know.

---

[v] Reifies means makes it into a god. It elevates in status, making it seem concrete and real.

[vi] I first encountered this explanation of knowledge paradigms from reading and listening to critical theorist of education Joe L. Kincheloe.

The rules of the scientific method become a problem for intuition when we apply the rigorous standards of the scientific method to our lived experiences. Allegiance to objectivity in knowledge can make us second-guess our intuitive experiences. We look for proof or just generally question the validity—even of our own, lived experience.

A RATIONAL-ANALYTIC MINDSET DISTORTS OUR SELF-CONCEPT

When we recognize scientism as a belief, we see that what was once a *strategy* of objectivity and analysis has embedded the *value* of separation of self from everything else. Such separation effectively creates cognitive and emotional distance, seeding a sense of estrangement or alienation. Thinking of ourselves as separate—including separate from the world—has led to the development of cultural norms and practices that destroy our world…and ourselves. We feel disconnected from ourselves and each other. We feel disconnected from being rooted in a sense of place, from a feeling of purpose or meaning, or from a connection to something greater than ourselves.

One of the specific effects of scientism and of looking through a lens of mechanism over time is that we tend to read the world—and ultimately ourselves—as machine-like. Through the lens of science, all of reality is materially physical. The world is like a machine, made up of inanimate, non-conscious matter. Consciousness is nothing more than a result of activity in the brain. Minds are contained entirely in the brain, including images and memories.

The machine metaphor is so embedded, that beyond using mechanism as a metaphor, we start to believe that this is what we are. The language we often use to describe ourselves reflects that we think of *ourselves* mechanistically. Some of the psychology teachings describe our bodies and minds with language like 'hardwired;' someone unconventional might be labelled as having a 'screw loose.' The idea that machines are perfect or infallible and therefore more highly valuable than the flawed and often messy processes of humans and all organic beings has seeped into and formed our culture so thoroughly that we unconsciously prioritize mechanistic ways of being—without realizing that we don't work that way.

When we treat ourselves as machine-like, we assume that bodies and psyches—just like machines—should be predictable. And then we can become frustrated when people don't live up to mechanistic standards of productivity and orderly perfection. We might believe in the superiority of linear, progressive development, and expect that certain input should reap a predictably certain output. You might even be hoping that cultivating your intuition can help you be more productive or efficient. Spoiler alert: As organisms (not mechanisms), it doesn't quite work that way.

Because the scientific paradigm focuses on problems that can be seen, it tends to address problems of the outer world. This, too, is reflected in how we have tried to understand ourselves, and especially, our minds. Through the lens of scientism, the mind and body are separate operations, with the mind doing the complex and important work and the body only playing a supportive role to cognitive processing. The thinking mind is elevated, while the feeling, sensing body is understood as a container for consciousness rather than being integral to consciousness. This hierarchy is embedded in the belief that the brain is the *cause* of experience, with consciousness being the result of biological, chemical processes originating in the brain. (Or possibly, per more recent developments, throughout the body, such as in the gut.)

Within a modality like psychology where so many experts think of consciousness as a result of neurobiological processes, psychic intuition is simply incomprehensible. Analytic science makes it seem as if only waking, ordinary consciousness is worth knowing about,[42] while dream states, meditative states, and other non-ordinary states of consciousness are not. Instead, the psyche gets framed as a shadowy and untrustworthy terrain, and a gap in understanding intuitive experience remains because it is understudied.

In these & other ways, the analytic mode denies a connected, holistic experience of living that extends to our relationships with energy, our bodies, and the unseen world of the transpersonal realm. It doubles down on an outlook that severs us from ourselves and our world, dismissing our lived experience in favour of authorized knowledge, a form of collective gaslighting.

As a process for making sense of the world, analysis takes things apart to understand them, breaking things down into components. Its approach to knowledge is to name, measure, and delineate categories and boundaries that define *this* is not *that*. In many cases, we equate this analysis with knowing. There's an underlying belief that words or categories can accurately represent the underlying structure of our world. We point to a thing (name it, triangulate it) and think we know it[vii]. The reverse is true, too: If we can't point to it, we think it's most likely made up.

As a result, we tend to disavow all kinds of experience that can't be seen or categorized neatly, and undervalue whatever is unconscious, uncanny, or uncomfortable. Unexplained or unseen phenomena get categorized as unreal, which makes some topics (like psychic intuition) taboo. We avoid mentioning them, and we don't know how to talk about them without risking our 'respectability.'

Of course, putting something into words doesn't make it real or true. Not everything that is valuable can be put into words. There are other valid ways of experiencing things besides *thinking* about them. Modalities like art, mythology, poetry, and dreams are all ways of representing non-discursive experience. They can point to what is true, even if they don't make sense in the objective-analytic-rational standard of 'sense.'

As we saw in Chapter 3, intuitive experiences abide by their own kind of sense; their own non-rational, non-discursive sense-making. But since intuition often happens at a level of consciousness before cognition and before language, we often miss hints, hunches, impressions, and even feelings. We don't recognize intuitive experience because we are trained to look for words and thoughts—which are external and concrete, or sensations—which are internal, but still tangible in some ways. Making a mindset shift to valuing intuition means that, when we have an intuitive

---

[vii] The English language, in particular, with its copious use of "to be" verbs, exemplifies how we tend to let language frame existence (be-ing) as static and stable rather than as emergent (be-coming). We tend to speak as if things simply are rather than as happening or as unfolding, emerging, or uncertain. We say: "I am. Things are." In this way, we have embedded a collective habit of speaking our belief in fixity and objectivity into existence.

experience, even if it doesn't make rational sense, we can begin to trust it. (Remember, intuition is embodied and holistic. It doesn't happen without the whole mind-body package).

No matter how embedded analysis is in our language and in our thinking, experiences do not necessarily begin and end neatly. Analysis can't account for the complex, holistic nature of human experience. It can't account for the unseen creative principle that animates all living systems. And because of this orientation, analysis is ill-suited to understanding organism and anything else unpredictable, uncertain, flowing, changing, and interconnected.

This is why it's a mistake to try to understand intuition from within a framework of analysis and scientific principles. When we do, we end up with a misconception.

THE SECOND MISTAKE, MYSTIFICATION, IS A TWIST

The mindset mistake of mystification is a different twist on trying to make intuition respectable or comprehensible according to the rational-analytic framework. It's another response to the same problem: trying to understand intuition from outside an intuitive logic. Mystification means hiding, obscuring, or even distorting what something is. In ordinary language, to *mystify* means to perplex or confuse. In sociological theory, mystification is the distortion of perception, where we create and perpetuate a story about something to avoid seeing it as it is.

And the distorted story we tell about intuition? The veil of mystification hides that intuition is a normal experience, accessible to anyone. We mystify intuition by making it seem so special and magical that you have to be a certain type of way or have a certain kind of ability or identity to access it. It's a form of idealization.

We see this in the tendency to construct intuition as perfect or transcendent. We hear it in descriptions of intuitive experience as 'direct downloads' from a divine source rather than an innate human capacity. We hear it in the way intuition gets described as always, perfectly correct, and never ever wrong. And that if it's wrong, it wasn't intuition (a claim made by Romantic philosophers and New Agers[viii] alike).

The mystifying narrative goes a little something like this: Intuition is so special and so amazing we couldn't possibly explain it, other than through a religious or spiritual lens. In the same vein as god, spirit, or other entities you might believe in, intuition simply *is:* perfect and unassailable. Although this framing can sound like reverence, it actually works to delegitimize intuitive experience. Intuition becomes a matter of belief, not knowledge. Mystification is a way of saying: If we can't possibly understand, describe, or define it, that's because it might not be real.

Mystifying intuition as 'only perfect' certainly complicates our relationship to it. It makes intuition too special, which acts as a barrier that prevents people from realizing when they're experiencing it. There's a whole story about what intuition is supposed to look like or feel like. Sudden, dramatic, and absolutely certain, for example. Because of mystification, we internalize the idea that we should all experience intuition that way. We expect intuitive experience to have a particular form, and if it doesn't? We're simply not intuitive. This means many of us don't get to trust that we can access intuition, often because we don't know what intuitive experience can feel like, outside of that idealized version.

[viii] For example, transpersonal psychologist Frances E. Vaughan makes this claim in *Awakening Intuition* (1979).

As a mindset issue, we're more likely to doubt ourselves if we don't identify as the type of intuitive person we have in mind, or if our intuitive experiences don't show up the way we're expecting them to. We already do doubt our intuitive experiences so much. For example, how many times have you heard (or said) something like, "This might sound crazy, but…" or "Don't think I'm weird, but…?" These phrases minimize our right to rely on the authority of our intuitive knowing.

The mindset mistake of mystification leads to the widespread habit of framing intuition as a *source* of information. We personify something called Intuition, an all-knowing agent of knowledge we can tap into. This misunderstanding stems from the assumption that knowledge is (or should be) objective. It doesn't require a context that the knower exists in; the knower should be able to transcend their context to make direct contact with this perfect source of knowing, Intuition.

This framing ignores that intuition is a process or a relationship between parts of ourselves. It leaves out us—the agent of experience and the subject of knowing—and glosses over our agency in this whole dynamic. Worse, it gives that agency over to something that gets referred to, generally, as our intuition. As if intuition itself is the source of the knowing. We get the impression that intuition should be something we own, like a tool.

Here, it's worth remembering intuition on its own terms, as an experience, process, or relationship. Mystification conveniently leaves out that intuitive experience is a relationship between a person and the grander forces of potential, creation, coherence, and synthesis. It doesn't happen *to* us but *within* and *through* us, despite how it sometimes feels.

Mystification becomes a problem because claiming intuition as perfect, infallible, or divine ignores that the objectively perfect intuitive content (if it even was perfect) is always experienced and translated through imperfect, subjective, human awareness. The content may arrive directly, but it still gets processed through the (flawed, human) filters of emotions, thoughts, reasoning, and analysis. It can seem like intuitive experience is unattainable, leading us to ignore how intuition and analysis work together.

Mystification leads us to believe that all intuition is extra-ordinary. When, more accurately, intuition is a useful, normal, valuable part of human consciousness.

The trouble with describing psychic intuition as *extra*sensory or *extra*-ordinary is that the emphasis on "extra" makes it seem like intuition is something we experience only if we're lucky or in an emergency or as something only those with a so-called gift can access. Making intuition extra-magical is an expression of separation or alienation. It's a mindset that creates distance between us and intuitive experience.

Now, intuition does point us toward some strange, multidimensional phenomena that we don't always have language for. We often call it wacky or woo-woo as a placeholder. And after hundreds of years parking the emotions, intuition, and the inner dimensions of consciousness with religion, we have a diminished capacity for knowing how to think (let alone talk) about them. We also lack language for a concept of energetic flow, and for the exchange of information in unseen realms. But as we know, just because something exists outside of the verbal realm does not mean it's not relevant to our mundane lives. Mystification has led to a lax understanding of what intuition is, what human consciousness is capable of, and even of what we are. To overcome this mindset issue, we likely need to more carefully consider what we believe, and reckon with our mythic and symbolic structures and the metaphors we have available to us.

WOMEN'S INTUITION, MYSTIFICATION, AND POWER

Many of us still believe intuition is something that rightfully belongs to psychics, mystics, freaks, witches, and certain of our wacky, woo friends. As if it's not an ability we all have a connection to.

When intuition gets relegated to distinct, specific groups, the woo aspects of intuitive experience become sort of tolerable—but only because it belongs to contained categories of people. Its like saying, intuition happens, but it's not universal and it's definitely not normal. As if containing these experiences in a packet belonging to only one group of people makes its existence somehow more acceptable. Through mystification, we allow intuition to be mystical, but limit its expression, put in a box meant for Those People; eccentric Others. Intuition is for *them*, over there, but not us.

When we mystify intuition by thinking of it as a special ability that only some special people have, that becomes an issue of power. It gatekeeps *who* is allowed to know (not only intuitively, but in general) and who is prevented from claiming knowledge, as well as which *ways* of knowing are allowed and authorized and which are dismissed as 'folklore' or mere imagination. This aspect of mystification is a legacy of how, at a certain point in modern history, religions were given domain over everything 'spiritual.' Inner knowing became reserved for mystics and miracles, supposedly inaccessible to everyday people—except for priests.

The question of power and authority is complicated by a specific form of mystification: claims to women's or mother's intuition.[ix]

On the surface, mystification doesn't seem like a problem. In certain cultural corners, we can find many examples of (usually) women who even trade on this special ability—for example, in New Age 'goddess' traditions, where it is not uncommon to suggest that intuition is innate and unique to women. Many of the new age self help books and courses that teach intuition development explicitly claim intuition to be a special, 'feminine' superpower. These women are using mystification to claim psychic intuition *for* women. And, while some women—who have traditionally been denied authority as 'knowers'—may feel empowered by claiming intuition for women, it's not enough to let only *some* people experience intuition on its own terms; doing this still perpetuates the mindset that intuition is only accessible to some people, in some circumstances.

Mother's intuition is a particular form of specialness; we think there's some ability granted to mothers. And there is some truth to the idea. Mothers tend to be highly attuned to their children. They can often sense what their children need, without any manifest evidence. Birthing mothers are also biologically connected to their children, heightening the connection through hormonal—and possibly chromosomal—interactions that persist beyond birth.

---

ix   For much more about mother's intuition, you can find a research article I wrote about it at www.WhatisIntuition.ca

Aside from the mother-child connection, women tend to be socialized in ways that support intuitive development. We learn to be especially attuned to others' needs. We often maintain a generalized vigilance of our environments, scanning for safety. Generally, people who are raised to be girls and women are socialized to pay attention inward and to others, to be aware of their surroundings, to be empathic, and to register feelings in the body, all habits that might amplify intuitive experience.

However, claiming that intuition is the special domain of women (or yes, even mothers) is problematic in its assumptions about gender. Linking intuition exclusively to women perpetuates an essentialized version of femininity. So, even when it's positioned as a compliment or an elevation, within patriarchal culture, this claim relies on a binary that equates women with the body and emotions and men with reasoning and the mind. Within this discourse, women's or mother's intuition is viewed as less significant or meaningful compared to the version of intuition that relies on fast thinking or even the more concrete gut feeling, with its definitive sensory accompaniment. Somehow, gut feelings seem more trustworthy than the less-tangible experiences of clairsentience, claircognizance, or 'just knowing,' which are more commonly reported ways mother's intuition gets experienced.

Sometimes, a similar mystifying discourse about women's intuition is applied to children. We idealize children and their ability to be—and know—authentically. It's probably true that children are more intuitive than adults, likely because we all start out with a robust connection to the inner voice. But intuition is educated out of us in schools and socialized out of us by cultural norms. There are so many ways we are turned away from intuitive capacity by society—the requirement in school to show our work;

telling children "Oh, you're just imagining that;" or idealizing reason and the thinking mind. Like we do with women, we simultaneously idealize and marginalize children, too. Their access to special knowledge like intuition, is only permissible because they don't hold any real power.

Intuition doesn't need to be mystified in order to be special. Intuition *is* special, but it's not exclusive. It need not be reserved for mothers, or professional psychics, or that one person on your team at work who has a knack for getting the marketing strategy just right. It also doesn't only arise in special circumstances or extreme situations (although we might become more aware of it in those moments). On the contrary: intuition on its own terms can be a source of information about any aspect of experience.

A SUMMARY OF THE METAPHYSICAL CHOICE TO PRIORITIZE ANALYSIS

By now, it should be clear why the intuitive mode has remained such a mystery to us. Its value has been mystified and misunderstood by a dominant culture that has upheld the rational-intellectual-analytic mode as the only way to know. Meanwhile, the intuitive mode is cloistered away, not to be spoken of except behind closed doors, and knowledge that isn't experienced as coming through the rational modes is easily dismissed. It *has* to be, since it has no place within the dominant, analytic framework.

But that framework is wildly outgrown. Intuition is not merely cognitive. And while intuitive experience can take many forms, most generally intuition is a state of relatedness, a mode of connection, or a function of resonance. We can experience intuition because human consciousness extends beyond material and objective gestures to sense energy, vibrations, and affect.

In order to trust intuition on its own terms, we have to take on a mindset that values intuitive experience. This intentional cultivating is necessary because, as a consequence of the hegemony of the intellectual-analytic paradigm, we have become alienated from our own intuitive experience. We tend to believe that the linear, visible world—that can be named, labelled, bought, and sold—is the 'real' world and that the unseen world is, at best, superstitious or, at worst, a phantom of the imagination.

As a result of long-term dominance of the rational-analytic mode, we are habituated to expect knowledge to arrive in a rational, binary, hierarchical, and linear way. And if it doesn't, we assume it must be coming from some magical, unreachable, transcendent source. Sometimes we idealize and over-value it, and other times we dismiss and devalue it. Both of these are responses to interpreting intuition from within an analytic, binary lens.

The two different mindset 'mistakes'—misconception and mystification—create a barrier of separation between ourselves and intuitive experience that replicates the ethos of separation and individualization embedded in scientism and its analytic-rational-binary logic.

For some of us, to the extent that we're invested in a binary framework, this separation might be the only way we can be okay with intuition—meaning, it somehow makes it totally fine to have woo-woo experiences as long as they have a clearly identifiable source (especially if it can be connected to a 'legitimate' religious source). For others, this separation is itself a barrier to experience and deprives us of taking ownership of the experience, another form of alienation.

Resolving the problems of mystification and misunderstanding requires us to shift how we choose to relate to our lived experiences, especially those that are difficult or impossible to put into words or conceptualize as ideas. A belief in divine intervention or the angelic realm should not be required for conceptualizing intuition; the depth of relatedness and connectedness that psychic intuition reveals is profound enough, without involving a godhead or angelic intervention.

I want us to value these kinds of experiences for what they are: transpersonal, non-discursive intelligence. With this desire, I am aligning with many of the wisdom traditions that have turned inward for information, knowledge, and truth. Taking our own, lived experiences as a starting point, we can attune our attention so that we can experience more of whatever we sense intuitively.

To make this shift in understanding and start to value intuition as a mode of producing knowledge (and try to understand intuition on its own terms), we need to expand our framework of reality. If psychic intuition can't make sense within the window we're looking out of, we need a bigger window. Or maybe, we need a full renovation of our house of belief.

PRACTICES FOR MINDSET

How do we move from the mindset we learned growing up to a mindset that is more open, more willing to value other perspectives, more oriented to inner experiences?

How do we move towards making metaphysical choices that align with *intuition on its own terms*?

The practices that help us shift mindset include:

Consuming media that introduce us to ideas that confront the binary analytic worldview. You're already well on your way by reading this book, asking these questions, being challenged on these issues, challenging your assumptions, and reckoning with what you think you're doing here and what all of this is.

Shifting our perspective. Learning through stories, taking a step back for a wider view, or a step towards, for a closer look. Considering alternative choices and constructions about the nature of reality. After all, what are beliefs but metaphysical choices we have made about how we understand the world?

Discovering the beliefs we already have about intuition, interrogating whether those beliefs reflect our lived experience, and then doing what's necessary to update those beliefs as needed. Once you can recognize what you think intuition is, you can start shifting your mindset.

It may help to remember that intuition is not a skill; it is a way—an approach—of knowing and being. In other words, intuition is a way of inhabiting ourselves and our lives that starts from accepting intuition on its own terms. Accommodating that is the first step in cultivating our relationship with the intuitive self.

Here's the thing: We have to intentionally practice an open, intuitive, receptive mindset. We have to practice curiosity and show up with a willingness to be uncertain—even if only for a moment. We have to be willing to entertain the idea that (especially nonlocal and psychic) intuitive experience is possible.

When we're practicing the work of the mindset pillar, we can expect to kick off a recursive feedback process. Experiencing the holistic-intuitive mode as real gives us reason to be receptive to energy and intuitive experience, and preparing our minds for these experiences makes them more likely to occur.

INTERROGATING BELIEFS

Perhaps start here: What has challenged you about what you have read so far? Do you value reason and analysis over intuition or emotion? Are you invested in the special power of women to be more intuitive? Do you assign an external source to the intuitive experiences you have?

What do you believe about consciousness? Intuition? The nature of spirit? What's your relationship to the unseen dimensions?

Answering these questions will require a fair bit of introspection.

Framing intuition on its own terms, as an experience (rather than as a source or a skill) reminds us that the knower can't be taken out of the equation. We're needed in the dynamic to perceive and translate the intuitive content. We know that so many of us can't be trusted with this task since our assumptions about the psychic realm, about consciousness, about our own abilities have already limited us. But it's also not sufficient to just say that intuition is always perfect, and therefore whatever I say, as long as I claim it as intuition, is right. Tricky, this.

We need to allow for complexity and the both/and logic. For example, we can choose to wholeheartedly consider the belief that everything is energy and decide to recognize energy as the stuff of the subatomic universe and *also* acknowledge that there is a solid, material plane that we all live within. Even if the quantum reality means that a table is more energy than solid, we still *experience* it as solid, so the energy aspect is only partially relevant to everyday experience. We can keep the energy realm in mind and rely on it for perspective, but we can also still presume that, when we set that table for dinner, the plates and silverware will stay where we place them.

OVERCOMING MISCONCEPTION AND MYSTIFICATION

It might seem strange that I want to point out the limitations of mystification. My own intuitive function was activated by a reiki attunement, and I have an intimate relationship with energy and the unseen world. But getting on board with our beliefs is part of making intuition accessible; it's about affirming intuitive experiences that don't conform or correspond to the idealized version that many of us have internalized as the 'right' way to be intuitive (i.e., clairvoyant, with guides, etc.).

It's hard to do this with an experience so internal and subjective. Sometimes it's so subtle we don't know if we're having it or not!

Even where scientific and philosophic lineages can account for psychic experience to some extent, we still get uneasy around this stuff. Many of us have grown up with the idea that intuitive experience is freaky, witchy, unwelcome, or something to hide, if not suppress. This is a form of colonization of our minds. Intuition gets covered up, denied existence, and is replaced by a dominant, hegemonic approach that ultimately is not in our own interests but has become something we carry within us and perpetuate.

Ask yourself: in what ways do you buy into the misconception that there's a boundary around acceptable intuition or fast thinking, making it somehow more trustworthy than other forms of intuitive experience?

INVESTING IN TRUST ON PURPOSE

Next, we dig out our internalized skepticism of intuition and the intuitive mode, making it acceptable to say to ourselves and to others, "Yep, I know this intuitively." We replace skepticism with the experiential belief that intuition is a valid mode of knowing.

For those of us raised in a culture dominated by scientism and materialism, experiencing intuition as an act of trust rather than fear or doubt likely will not come naturally. For us, it's too simple to say that we should trust our intuition. Before that trust can happen, we have to *unlearn* our internalized default to doubt.

An overemphasis on doubt and skepticism leads us to distrust ourselves because we believe that it is more correct to doubt than to trust. Study after psychological study tell us why we shouldn't trust ourselves. They explain all the ways our minds deceive us, and we internalize this belief. Doubt culture is especially apparent in our collective preference for things to be fixed and stable, which is connected to an existential preference for believing that life is certain. Yet when we're too tightly invested in predictable outcomes and expectations, we become more likely to overlook or ignore intuitive experience.

Intuitive experience is supported by being comfortable with uncertainty, because even though some intuitive hits feel certain inside, there's often a delay before the outcome of an intuitive hit becomes clear. To counteract the default of modern culture's doubt is to practice allowing for uncertainty. The uncertainty of the intuitive mode requires trust in the process—as process itself (rather than being fixated on an outcome). Often, there's no proof, and there's no universal playbook for how to receive intuitive experience, other than the one that evolves from subjective experience. So we track our experience by keeping an intuition diary. We record intuitive hits and impressions. We can then return to these notes later to confirm. (More on this later.)

By embracing uncertainty and a certain amount of fuzziness, on purpose, we can infuse an attitude of trust into our own experiences.

Trust and receptivity are choices we can make. Choosing to trust our experience makes it possible to remain open and receptive and makes it increasingly likely that we will be more aware of our intuitive experiences, even if they are fuzzy, unclear, or (as intuition most often is) non-discursive. We can trust that something is real even if it doesn't appear as we might have expected it to. In this way, the scope of what is 'real' and 'true' can be opened up so that subjective experiences like dreams, feelings, and psychic awareness can be considered trustworthy and valued—not as mere myth nor merely personal individual quirks but sources and repositories of *knowledge*.

Let's clarify the logic of this practice. Taking on an attitude of trust instead of defaulting to doubt won't necessarily happen just by deciding to do it, not after lifetimes of protective measures against naive trust. Nor would I suggest that people can just change their outlook about this on a dime, without investing in self-awareness and mindfulness about this shift. Intelligent trust is a practice that has to be nurtured. And we'll discuss this more thoroughly in chapter 7, on Discernment.

The pursuit of transforming your mindset is a radical practice of examining what we perceive, think, and desire, since what we pay attention to conditions what we notice. Likewise, what we're conditioned to notice becomes what we pay attention to. So, although it seems simple to say intuition is enhanced by paying attention (the essence of Pillar 2, Awareness), this is an important and transformative piece of advice that is driven by mindset, attitude, and belief about what can be experienced. Cultivating your intuition is a reclamation of psychic freedom and an expanded range of experience, enabled by this shift in mindset.

Chapter 6

PILLAR 2: AWARENESS

The intuitive mode begs us to stop viewing our world through the metaphor of mechanism. Our world is made up of living systems; vibrating interactions! It's more space than solid, and more dynamic than static. The universe (multiverse, really) is comprised of infinite sources of conscious, potential energy that coheres and dissolves in various configurations and relations. And in intuitive moments, we can capture some of that potential as informational content.

That's how intuition makes sense on its own terms.

As we move on from cultivating the state of mind that supports us being intuitive, how do we integrate this understanding? In Pillar 2, we get our body and attention on board to anchor in the receptive state most likely to facilitate intuitive awareness. We learn to tune in to the body, both physical and energetic, experiencing that these carry and hold information. We practice cultivating a flow state that is more aware of both outer and inner contexts (especially inner, since that needs more practice). We attend to the practical work that lets us get to know intuition on its own terms—cultivating receptive awareness, developing sensitivity, and paying attention to the embodied expression of intuitive experience.

In the intuitive mode, we know something by aligning or resonating with the thing being known. And so all intuitive practice begins with aligning to ourselves.

In this pillar, we teach ourselves (and allow ourselves) to become more sensitive and attentive to vibes (energetic, emotional, etc.) and tune our consciousness to experience more of what there is to experience. This is where we practice paying attention to our thoughts, emotions, cravings, and other signals of all kinds from the body. This intentional practice helps us inhabit a sense of intuitive connection, beyond or outside of thought. With practice, we develop a feedback loop of listening and paying attention, tuning in to notice what's there to notice and then noticing even more.

Here, we're challenged to recognize that our minds, bodies, and spirits are interconnected with everything else in ways that we don't usually recognize (both in the sense that we don't typically pay attention to it and that we don't often acknowledge as real). We integrate the idea that individual consciousness is an aspect of collective or universal consciousness, the prima materia of life. And we get to experience that interconnection through the body and its various organs of perception, beyond the five 'ordinary' senses.

To get started, let's review some key concepts:

- Intuition is inner-directed awareness. It's unmediated perception and apprehension (taking in sensory awareness/figuring something out). It's sudden recognition.
- Intuition engages us directly with realms of consciousness that we don't always attend to consciously. So, in this pillar of cultivating intuition, we focus our attention towards letting in more content, specifically from the unseen dimensions.
- The fact of intuitive experience reveals that we are ultimately much more connected than our daily experiences let on or that our rational-analytic culture admits.
- The brain filters information simply because there would otherwise be way too much input. With intention and practice, we can change how—and how much—we pay attention. We can shift the lens we use to perceive, so that different kinds of information filter through.
- We can perceive in the nonphysical realm. Thoughts, ideas, vibes, moods, and affect are all around.

- It's possible to perceive energy itself. Just as my intuitive sense was heightened after becoming attuned to reiki energy, when our energetic field is more coherent, we can be both receptive and self-contained.
- Through a path of practice based in cultivating self-awareness and mindfulness, we can learn to perceive, interpret, and then act on intuitive experience.

What we do and don't perceive, see, or notice is framed by many factors, including mindset (what we expect to exist) and our unique sensory capabilities. By practicing a *stance* of attention and an openness to noticing, we make new perception possible. In Pillar 2, we exercise those capabilities, practicing and playing with the limits of what we make ourselves available for.

PAYING ATTENTION

Pillar 2 is all about cultivating awareness. Paying attention to non-discursive experience like intuition is a skill we can cultivate through meditation and other mind-body practices where we focus directly (usually on the breath) instead of focusing on the constant stream of thoughts, ideas, and concepts that typically run through our awareness. This work helps us to heighten awareness of the inner experiences we typically let slip by.

Practices of mindful attention and awareness help us pay more attention in general. They reduce stress, distractions, and the limiting interference of the logical mind, which tends to play the role of censor in the psyche. And, it's easier to pay attention inward when the mind is quiet.

The practices for cultivating intuition draw us into deeper connection and into a greater awareness of that connection. We become aware—and then aware of our awareness. With that awareness of awareness, we begin to perceive more intuitive content and recognize a greater depth and breadth of interconnectedness.

Although it seems simple to advise that intuition is enhanced by paying attention, this is an important and transformative piece of advice that is driven by mindset, attitude, and belief about what we can experience. To put it bluntly, if you don't believe you can be intuitive, you will not let yourself be aware of intuitive input, information, or awareness. The mindset pillar has helped us become more aware of the metaphysical choices we make all the time. Now, we continue to enlarge the lens with which we perceive, judge, and filter experience.

This work is a reclamation of psychic freedom, designed to make us more aware of an unseen connection that is already there. We bring that awareness closer to the fore, working to integrate the mind, body, and spiritual realms.

If this sounds simple, know that it can be deceptively difficult. For one thing, most of us are out of practice, having been taught and encouraged to not do this kind of introspective, critical work. In fact, we're mostly oriented in the wrong direction. Rather than tune in, we learn to tune out.

It can be really uncomfortable to examine ourselves as we are and to inquire about how we have come to be that way. Some of this is painful and some just cringe-y. Many of us spend every waking moment studiously avoiding relating to ourselves with this much attention.[i] The impulse to avoid looking inward and paying attention to the simple experience of *being* is strong and is reinforced by our culture. Yet that is what intuition development requires. We need to prioritize introspective and contemplative practice and learn to trust that these practices can generate knowledge and expanded awareness.

The mindset pillar helps us change our thoughts. But changing our actual perception? That takes further practice. We have to get ourselves into the receptive mode and then play around in there. We need to expand our expectations of how intuitive experience can show up. Because often, it's not in our thoughts but in our bodies. And sometimes, it's not even in the body; we are just presented with intuitive content: a sudden awareness, a spontaneous image or thought.

There is a lot we can pay attention to, and while I'm definitely not advocating for hypervigilance, I am suggesting that we open to the opportunity for intuitive experience by deepening and widening our scope of attention.

You see, attention exists on a spectrum. We make assumptions about what there is to notice based on our perspective, identity, cultural imprints, and other filters. Through intuition development, we also cultivate awareness of (and learn to pay attention to) what is going on outside and around us—our context, relationships, connections, and the world at large, including both the seen and the unseen dimensions. To correct an imbalance, we pay particular

---

i You might have heard about the psychological experiment that demonstrated how people would rather shock themselves with an electronic paddle than think quietly alone for a number of minutes. I'm not kidding when I say that introspection and paying attention to ourselves is difficult.

attention inward, to our embodied experience, including thoughts, emotions, feelings, and responses.

When we do start to pay more attention, we might find that our contexts are more complex than we are normally aware of. We need boundaries around our attention; that's a role of consciousness. These keep us sane! But our boundaries themselves need to be examined regularly, lest they become too rigid. If we boundary too hard, intuition can't break through.

Intuitive experience is best served by a dispersed quality of consciousness, meaning that you can't look too hard. Remember: focusing is a limiting practice. It's like looking at the sky during a meteor shower. If you focus on any one star, or even any one area of the sky, you're likely to miss a shooting star. But when you de-focus and gaze out at the sky as a whole, you're far more likely to catch a glimpse of the moving meteors.

Instead of looking too hard, we cultivate a receptivity that is oriented to potential and possibility. In this way, the practice of intuition development works to entrain our awareness so we can be in this receptive state more often. The balance point is like the state of relaxed attention brought about in contemplative states. We might call this an inner state of *surrender*.

PRACTICES FOR AWARENESS

Developing receptive awareness requires us to pay attention to the following:

Attention to self. There are so many things to notice about ourselves (especially with a holistic idea of what the self entails (mind, body, spirit, and intra-active, conscious engagement). We develop awareness of our embodied experiences and our tells. This can start with paying attention to cues like hunger and thirst, even bathroom cues.

Inner self-awareness. We map previous intuitive experience to create a blueprint for what it feels like for us. We notice the tendencies and habits of our minds and stay curious about thoughts, fears, inner censorship, and things we ignore (or pretend) about ourselves.

Outer self-awareness. We pay attention to our environment and the interactions taking place within it—seen and unseen—including energetic aspects, shifts, and clues in the environment. We develop our sensory capabilities (including extra-sensory ones) and let our attention take in a wider range of input.

Interpersonal/relational context. We learn to notice our empathic intuition. We feel into others' vibes, moods, and emotions. And we identify our emotional tells.

Holistic context. We attend to the transpersonal and unseen features of experience. We develop energy sensitivity and notice resonance in the subtle body through vibes and coherence with energies that hold information. We expand our heart's capacity as an organ of perception.

FLOW STATE

Most of us become aware of intuitive experience when it spontaneously arises to a consciousness that is otherwise occupied, when our attention is not tightly focused, but diffuse. Consciousness is more receptive to intuition in moments when we're doing something else, like when we are caught up in ordinary, everyday tasks. These spontaneous scenarios are described in creativity literature as the 'bed-bath-bus' phenomenon (the locations where such insights often occur). These are moments when inspiration hits because we are calmly distracted, relaxed, and engaged in the flow of doing something else. (You've had those sudden 'aha' moments of intense clarity in the shower, right? Yep, that's what I'm talking about.)

A relaxed-yet-attentive state of awareness can give rise to the optimal experience of *flow*,[43] which is known to support intuition and other aha moments—where all of a sudden, there is coherence. Everything (or just something) makes sense.

Flow is a state in which we are completely immersed in our experience—think of athletes during a game or musicians when they lose themselves in performance.

We can intentionally cultivate such clear-headed moments. When we pause to specifically relax the mind from a problem we've been working on, a receptive state generally arises. This is a strategy sometimes called incubation, letting the problem gestate while we carry on. We can support incubation by getting up and doing something else: taking a walk, cooking or baking, doodling, journaling, or anything else that distracts the thinking mind so the rest of our consciousness can relax and activate a creative response. Although it might seem counterintuitive in the context of a high-stress lifestyle, we can enable flow by scheduling in some unstructured time in the day to relax the intellect and become more open to receptive awareness.

COHERENCE

We are most intuitive and in tune when our brains, bodies, and hearts are coherent, vibrating on the same wavelength. So, in general, cultivating awareness is a process of becoming increasingly coherent, by surrendering to the dynamic flux of our experience. Centring, grounding, and clarifying boundaries are the foundations of this work.

Coherence is facilitated by mental, physical, and emotional well-being, as it's easier to receive (or perceive) subtle experience when we are balanced and at ease. When we are coherent in this sense, the nervous system, the immune system, the cardiovascular system, and the hormonal system are all working together in harmony. These factors support intuitive knowing by allowing us to experience increased energetic flow, facilitating communication and interaction between the mind, body, and spirit.

In a coherent state, energy is used efficiently. Psychologically, we feel less tension and more flow in our experience, facilitating the relaxed, receptive awareness in which intuition arises more easily. We become more aware of and open to the energy around us, creating space for intuitive hits.

There are many techniques and behaviours that help cultivate coherence and that open the subtle body, facilitate experiences of flow, and support resonance. A whole range of mind-body practices exist for this: regulating the nervous system, smoothing the aura, and cultivating inner resources (inner fire). Cross-culturally, practices for restoring balance include mindful movement, purification techniques, cultivating silence and stillness, prayer, invocation, setting intentions, making offerings, sacrifice, and expressing gratitude. I recommend taking up whichever of these practices resonates, to become more centred and grounded as you set out on the path of cultivating intuitive awareness.

SENSORY AND EXTRA-SENSORY PERCEPTION

So many intuitive experiences get discounted as something other than intuition. Say you always get the same uncanny feeling at a certain person's house or in a particular shop. We might discount it, saying, "Yeah, I felt that, but I always feel that here," not registering that that's intuitive information. Often, as a matter of cultural training and habit, we overlook the intuitive in the everyday and then only register the more intense, strange, or other-worldly intuitive experiences. This tendency is not only a profound disservice to our intuitive nature but also detaches us from paying attention to the subtle experiences in life, making our awareness duller and less connected.

Cultivating intuition includes developing progressively more subtle perception. Some vibes (for example certain ranges of light and sound waves) are perceptible by the usual five senses, while others are sensible in different ways. We know that the five senses don't cover all we can experience, and that human perception extends beyond these senses.[44] That's why we sort-of recognize ESP as a sixth sense, lumping much intuitive experience into this category. Extra-sensory includes the range of vibrations that we either can't usually perceive—or don't—out of habit.

The gut is starting to be more widely recognized as a centre of awareness in its own right, too, an organ of intelligence like the brain.[ii] (Of course, some cultures and wisdom traditions have known about the gut as an organ of perception and intelligence for a long time.) Gut feelings are a common, recognizable form of

---

ii   Neuroscientists recognize that the network of nerves throughout the digestive system is in constant contact with the brain. They even call this system, the enteric nervous system, a "second brain."

intuitive experience, which we can consider to be an activation of nerves. This is an instinctual connection, alerting us to danger or just the need to pay attention.

Information that occurs on subtle (energetic, etheric) levels is not usually 'sensed' in the ordinary meaning of that word—instead, as Jung noted, intuition may announce its presence through any (or none) of the senses. We call these manifestations, tells.

As we learned before, a tell is not the intuitive experience itself but a personal signal that draws your attention towards an intuitive experience. The key is to learn your personal tells so you know when something has meaning as intuitive experience—or not. We can cooperate by first registering that there's something to notice, then let the context relay information through the vibrosphere, and respond accordingly. Often, we ignore those tells and only recognize in hindsight that something was meaningful: "So that's what that was about" if we're lucky. Or more common, "I should have listened."

What we consider sensory or sensible is culturally conditioned. I don't know about you, but I grew up knowing unquestioningly that humans have five senses and I learned that these senses are simply how we experience the world. Nothing to question here. With intuitive sensing, there's no limit to the ways we might perceive it. If you're looking for a specific, generic tell, you might miss your hits.

As part of this work, you are encouraged to play and experiment. What does *your* intuition feel like? Do you get a gut feeling? Do you notice tension? Does your breathing change? Is there constriction in your throat? Does your body tingle, shiver, or flush? What are your tells? To identify this, our rational-linear orientation may need to be gently tucked away at first so that intuitive awareness can arise, away from the stern eye of the censoring mind.

And remember, intuition is a process, a mode, or way. Once we learn what it feels like, there's no need to point to it from the outside. With practice, we can start to lessen the need for asking, "Wait. Was that intuition? Or was that just fear, anxiety, wishful thinking, etc. etc. etc.?"

ENERGY BODY

I know about the energy body first-hand from my reiki practice, where we learn to intentionally cultivate the sensation of vibrations at the heart and other energy centres. We do this because we know, through inherited wisdom and experience, that energy is stored and moves through those areas of the body.

Reiki and other mind-body healing traditions have mapped and developed an understanding of the energy (etheric) body, and harness that knowledge for healing. I refer to reiki because it's a system I know, but there are lots of other practices and modalities that cultivate ki, or qi.[iii] This concept of energy and how it works through the body seems crucial to understanding how some intuitive experiences take place.

Because the concept of qi is so different from the Judeo-Christian understanding of energy and aliveness, it can be tempting to dismiss the existence of a universal life force energy and to reason away experiences of it. (Scientism at work!) The energetic body becomes coherent through practice. The process gets described

---

iii The English language does not really have an equivalent to the Eastern concept, qi, and so we more commonly borrow the word rather than translate it.

as smoothing the aura (i.e., field of energy)—getting rid of sticky spots or even gaping holes, those places where pain or trauma have left us with energetic scar tissue. These are places where healthy boundaries are not yet in place. (P.S. These are metaphors. But what they describe are also very, very real.)

Yoga is another example of making the energy body coherent through practice. *Asana* (posture practice) is a preparatory practice, not done just for body sculpting but for the purpose of enabling a deeper connection with the subtle energies of life. Yoga means 'union,' and the union envisioned was and is a conscious connection to the underlying foundational energetic consciousness that is the source and ground of all, both seen and unseen.

When the energetic body is coherent and energy is flowing well (i.e., it's neither stagnant nor in overdrive), we are more likely to experience the right amount of receptivity to perceive intuitive information. Just as we practice meditation to observe the flow of attention, energy work helps us refocus our attention so that we might notice non-material reality just as well.[iv]

Practices that support the subtle (energy) body and that help enhance intuition can include engaging with intentional energy practice through any movement, like yoga, reiki, tai chi, or qi gong; meditation; and visualization. Even a simple thing like sitting up straight will enhance energetic flow through the subtle body. (A straight spine lets blood, spinal fluid, and energy flow more freely

---

[iv] More and more, people are becoming aware of a sensitivity to energies. But there's a huge lack of mentorship and instruction about what to do with these awarenesses. Sometimes, acquiring sensitivity is uncomfortable. Sometimes it can coincide with other physical sensations, including pain. If you're finding yourself in a difficult spiritual emergence, please find a mentor or teacher.

through the body and to and from the brain. Try it now. Don't you feel more alert and vibrant?)

BOUNDARIES AND PERCEPTION

Intuitive experience does not rely on being excessively open and receptive. Receptive awareness depends on boundaries. This might seem contradictory, but because there is only so much we can take in as input, much of our sensory attention is limited or constrained to what is most necessary for survival in our complex, crowded world. When we establish more clearly defined boundaries around our attention, we can be more deliberate about the kind of information that gets into our conscious awareness. We can be intentional about awareness.

Let's think about how boundaries help us focus attention so that we perceive more of what we want to—and less of the clutter we need not pay attention to. Consciousness itself is a process of filtering and ordering too much information into coherent form so that we can make sense of what we experience. This has a dual function: allowing us to perceive in the first place, but also of limiting what we can perceive. For example, the way we limit our perception to the realm of objects—the seen world—is a result of educating ourselves to perceive (to filter) that way. After all, "to notice is to select,"[45] which raises the question of what we choose to notice. Maybe more importantly here: What governs what we choose to notice? And do we trust this part of ourselves? These choices are most often culturally conditioned. We need to become aware of our current existent boundaries. What do we let ourselves notice, see, know?

Here's a trivial example of how everyday consciousness acts as a filter and how easy it can sometimes be to change the filter. Several years ago, the eye doctor said I needed to wear glasses. I started the process of evaluating my prescription and shopping for frames. Suddenly (so it seemed), I noticed how many of my friends and family wear glasses. And strangers on the street! And in restaurants. It seemed that overnight everyone was now wearing glasses. Of course, the appearance of this seemingly overnight phenomenon across the entire population was caused entirely by my awareness. Now that eyeglasses were on my mind, my consciousness was filtering for them, whereas before it was likely filtering other people's eyeglasses out.

This is similar to how my relationship with intuition tends to intensify when I'm thinking about it. It has to do with how our attention works—amplifying and highlighting what's already there—and it illustrates how mindset functions…and why it matters. When we're paying attention to intuition, it shows up more.

As part of developing energetic coherence, boundaries help us fashion a container in which we can flow and respond in the ways we want. We decide what gets through. We determine how much output, how much input (and what kinds) we will accept. This helps us conserve and direct our most precious but limited resource: our energy, which is the conduit of our consciousness.

These days, we usually hear about boundaries as something we don't have enough of. We lack boundaries in terms of how we choose to direct our energy and spend our time. We are often expending energy where it isn't deserved or where we don't get it back to the degree we give it out. But cultivating intuitive awareness does involve a certain amount of permeability. It also requires us to strengthen boundaries where they matter: in keeping ourselves well and in maintaining our integrity.

Some of us do need to focus on relaxing our energetic boundaries, allowing more into awareness. As the science tells us, we're made up of more energy than matter, and we are inter- and intra-connected individuals. This way of understanding ourselves in relation to the world helps us decentre the egoic, individual self and lets us settle into becoming more comfortable and more connected to the context of our world and our relations. If we can learn to work *with* this interconnection, it becomes increasingly possible to perceive energy and energetic potential (like events that haven't happened yet).

But some might need tighter boundaries. Highly sensitive people often suffer from allowing too much into their sphere of awareness (consciously or unconsciously). If you identify as highly sensitive, you may benefit from learning how to become less open (when you want to rest) and from learning discernment practices that help you know which energies are which—which are personal, which are collective, which can (and should!) be left alone. You can set boundaries with visualization, with your intention, by keeping your energy body in good shape, or even by simply spending restorative time alone.

MEDITATION

When intuitive experience is unfamiliar, we need to practice using it, making it work, and familiarizing our whole mind-body system with what it sounds like, looks like, and feels like. Because attention is typically so focused outward, meditation, introspection, and fine-tuning our sensitivity are key.

Meditation is the most commonly recommended practice for stabilizing the development of intuition. You might say it's a fundamental prerequisite. The value of meditation lies in how it creates a receptive psychic environment. It cleans the slate, opens space, declutters. In fact, it's so effective that simply just taking up a regular meditation practice facilitates intuition development—whether or not cultivating intuition is an intended outcome. (I'm definitely more consciously intuitive when I've been doing my meditation practice more diligently.)

It's no coincidence that those who practice meditation or other contemplative practices are more comfortable in non-discursive realms. Wisdom traditions accept intuitive experience as a matter of fact, and as a valued mode of knowledge production. Hinduism, Buddhism, and other transpersonal lineages value, study, and seek out the inner realms of the psyche and the non-discursive experiences available therein. There is a dedicated interest about these inner realms as sources of knowledge, and practices honed over thousands of years help individuals access them. This has meant that lived, subjective experience (including non-ordinary experiences of consciousness) has been valued as an aspect of spiritual development rather than pathologized, as our Western culture tends to do.

Meanwhile, much of Western psychology has focused on studying behaviour and its observable, material causes. In general, Eurocentric psychology tends to pathologize the psyche and its extra-ordinary anomalies, leading us to avoid and even fear our own depths and innate abilities. We know that this has limited the possibilities for us to explore psychic experience, unless it fits within the narrow range of 'acceptable.' It has also left us without the skills and practices for inner exploration that help us get in there and know what is real within.

Paying attention to non-discursive experience is a skill we cultivate through meditation and other mind-body practices where we employ a direct focus on something like the breath to stabilize our focus and quieten the constant stream of thoughts, ideas, and concepts we're used to focusing on and that usually take up space in the mind.

What emerges from regular time with a quieted mind is enhanced intuitive access. The spontaneity and suddenness of intuitive insight means that intuition has not necessarily passed through the usual filters of thought. Through meditation practice, we begin loosening the filters, and the state that results from a quieted mind becomes a way to enhance intuitive access. Within that quiet, we can start to discern the various voices, messages, drives, and impulses that contribute to our conscious awareness. We become aware of awareness.

Centering during meditation: Centering is simply the act of placing ourselves in a position with nothing else to do but sit quietly and turn our attention inward, allowing the mind to defocus. It's a process of drawing within, to whatever you are experiencing at the time. The experience of centring, or coming to centre, is typically very relaxing. A kind of ease settles in, which is often accompanied by a plethora of pleasant sensations in the body and psyche. We tend to sit more upright, and we start to notice more (inward and/or outward).

When we first get quiet, an array of thoughts and feelings are likely to arise. It's important to avoid identifying these, lest we try to censor or control them. Instead, we aim to develop the stance of a neutral inner witness by quieting or distracting the mind through watching or counting breaths, visualizing an image, or simply gazing at a candle flame. A part of the mind is occupied by this focused attention. And—usually at the same time—thoughts come in. For the duration of the meditation, we acknowledge these but don't focus on them. The goal is to continually return the attention inward, to the sensation of breathing or whatever the chosen focus, and observe all the things taking place.

Inner Witness: Meditation supports an inner relationship of observation, or witnessing. The term 'inner witness' refers to the part of yourself that acts as an observer to the contents of the mind—thoughts, feelings, desires, etc. The inner witness is an aspect of the mind that observes the mind with some detachment from outcome. It can be a calm, unfazed, nonjudgmental presence in the midst of a thought-storm or emotional turmoil (or, let's be honest, just a regular day in the life of a post-modern mind).

In meditation, we practice being the witness by watching thoughts come and go while also maintaining focus on the meditative process. This allows for an interesting (albeit advanced) experience of self-ness: When you are able to watch yourself, it becomes possible to realize that what 'you' are is more than you might have thought. What you thought you were opens up and creates a new, expanded context for knowledge production.

Eventually, you recognize that 'you' are not the thinker. How can you be if you are also able to watch the thoughts? With practice, we become increasingly comfortable identifying more as the watcher of thoughts—the witness—than with the thoughts themselves, giving rise to an expanded perspective.

Inner Censor: The sibling of the witness-self is the inner censor. The censor is an internalized voice of doubt, educated by scientism, patriarchy, colonial-capitalism, religion, and other ideologies that seek to deny the power of liberated consciousness. Its job is to try and keep us safe, but it frequently overreaches. A primary effect of the censor is that it might not allow psychic experience to bubble up into awareness, so it stays at the level of affect or in the body, and the intuitive experience seems to lack content. In that way, the inner censor can hold us hostage, becoming a cause of stress or—over time—injury.

Buddhist practitioners speak of beginner's mind. This is a useful understanding that entails remaining receptive and curious, surrendering the expectation of mastery, and registering that practice is a permanent condition. It's about being patient. Allowing uncertainty. Allowing not-knowing. Receptive awareness is alert yet relaxed, curious but not striving, and meditation helps entrain the mind to be in this receptive state more often.

Through our meditation practice, we can transform our relationship to thought and judgment. We get to be aware without thinking. Most simply, the key to any intuition development practice is a quality of surrender. We learn to become responsive rather than reactive. We find that there is space between our thoughts and, with practice, can enlarge and elongate those spaces. Meditation helps us learn to allow the inner censor to rest. We learn to rest in that space, uncertain though it is.

A CAUTION ABOUT BYPASSING

Before I carry on, I feel I need to say that it's important that the relaxed, receptive attention of the intuitive stance is not a mind*less* one. It is mind*full*.

There is potential for great depth in this work, so be careful to take up a meditation practice that allows the work to touch the soul in a transformative way. This is not about love and light or the power of positivity. It's not about intent at all. Undertaking a practice that includes ideas and expectations can interfere with perceiving what is. It's much more about becoming a filter, and adjusting the spectrum of receptive awareness that filters what's really there.

And here I need to add a caveat about mindfulness practice and what gets called spiritual practice more broadly. Mindfulness has become a bit of a catchall practice, often introduced as an intervention for stress reduction or for improving behaviour (in schools) or productivity (in the workplace). In its popular forms, mindfulness practice sometimes stays at a surface level, enabling spiritual bypassing. While stress reduction and alleviating anxiety are important wellness goals and we should absolutely be incorporating them into our healthcare and education, in the wisdom traditions where it arose, mindfulness is a practice of gaining deep self-awareness and connection to the unseen. When taken up this way, as a spiritual practice, it can be messy, profound, transformative work that brings a deeper connection to your life because you're attending to the psyche and its depths.

Deepening the breath is great and can create much-needed relaxation. Paying attention to the experiences in the body during breathing practices, mindful movement (yoga, martial arts, other forms of exercise), dance, and play can light up the intuitive sensory dimension and will increase awareness of all kinds of other feelings and sensations in and through the body, signalling information we can use to be and stay well.

But having relaxation as the *goal* of mindful practice encourages us to glide over the stressors that created the tension in the first place. There are root causes that need to be addressed. In these cases, inner work can be glossed over in favour of a pleasant outcome or result. This is another reminder to get a mentor, teacher, or therapist to support you in cultivating your inner senses.

Spiritual practice is hard work! As we open up to see more of what is there, what arises is more light, sure, but also the awareness of more shadow. Psychic awareness is not necessarily nice or pleasant. We will know things we would normally choose to avoid knowing—things a less committed awareness might overlook. It takes both maturity and self-awareness to be receptive and secure enough to be willing to experience intuitive awareness. Opening up into a dynamic mode of receptive awareness is vulnerable. And, it's a commitment we don't always have to make. We get to put boundaries around our intuitive connection; we can develop agency to drop in and out.

Chapter 7

PILLAR 3: DISCERNMENT

The third pillar for cultivating intuition is the practice of discernment. Discernment, the ability to judge well, might not seem like something we should have to intentionally cultivate. We make deliberate choices all the time! But when we've been raised in a culture that prioritizes objective knowledge and outside authorities, it can be understandably hard to know how to trust our inner, subjective knowing. That's where discernment comes in.

Discernment is a path of practice that helps us become trustworthy knowers. In this pillar, we'll nurture our intuitive authority so that we develop the confidence to pay attention to—and believe in (and therefore act on)—our intuitive experience. By learning how and when to trust our intuition, we make it easier to act on intuition. We'll have fewer of those experiences where we only realize in retrospect that we knew…or should have known. We develop the authority and agency to know and to be intuitive knowers.

Discernment is cultivated by surrendering the (often automatic) defenses of the thinking-analytic mind and by developing an inventory of self-knowledge so that we are able to interpret, understand, and trust what we experience intuitively.

We come to know ourselves better by listening within, becoming familiar with our inner voices, memories, symbols, habits, and stories. When we start to pay attention inward, it turns out there is a lot going on in there! I liken this pillar to nurturing a relationship between parts of ourselves, letting some parts get louder while gently quieting others. We put the various parts of our self (representing different ways of knowing, and different approaches to attention, awareness, and keeping us safe) into a working relationship.

Discernment is a key to a bigger, political project about knowing: it requires that we put the person back into the story. Remember that how we understand 'self' matters to our mindset about intuition. There's the self we typically identify as; the person who other people also know, made up of personality, knowledge, memory, and other traits. Then there's the part of us that's connected to all else. Not just self, but Self. Plus, each of our selves are subject to the capabilities and limitations our embodiment brings.

What we think of as 'true' or 'valid' also matters here. Truth can refer to a static quality that requires everything else to be false (a binary take), or it can be understood in a nondual way that accepts that other things can also be true at the same time.

Culturally, we still have work to do to understand the subjective nature of knowledge (versus scientific objectivity), especially around the truth and validity of non-discursive experience. The Enlightenment's rules for science developed a method of validation that includes repeatability, where different methods or different observers should get the same result. This led to the notion that whatever is 'true' must be universally true.

However, as we know, knowledge acquired intuitively can't always be shared between people. Most intuitive experience cannot be confirmed through objective methodologies like double-blind experiments. It often can't be reported, charted, or signified since it relies on the sensory and interpretive functions of each individual for its meaning.

This doesn't mean that intuition is not worthy of trust. It just complicates our relationship to inner experience and the way we assess knowledge. Beyond scientism, trusting intuition on its own terms requires us to consider the value and validity of subjective knowledge production when it's deployed in a trustworthy way.

Note that I'm not advocating for *subjectivism*, the idea that every person is an expert of every subject and that just because a person thinks something, it is true. We can't just let any inner awareness stand as intuition. That's a recipe for utter disaster. Even though the requirement for objectivity in knowledge shouldn't apply to intuitive experience, that doesn't mean that anyone can say anything and it is true. (That's subjectivism.) Besides, something can be true for an individual, or true in the moment, and still not be universally true.

Intuition requires us to have a healthy amount of self-awareness, some expertise in the ways of our own minds. Instinct can function well without self-consciousness, but intuitive knowing depends on a self that is in conscious relationship with itself. From within, individuals can gauge the rightness of their intuition by relying on their intentionally developed, personal sense of awareness, discernment, and familiarity with symbolic meaning.

The practices in this pillar are oriented around developing a trustworthiness that comes from being self-aware, and doing ongoing self-reflection to be able to recognize the difference between intuition and other types of inner experience.

Discernment is how we make sense of intuitive content. It's how we interpret what's happening, what it means, and what to do about it. The more we can become self-aware and coherent, the more we recognize information flowing to and through us, and are better able to assess what that information means. We can learn to honour what we perceive, even when it doesn't (yet) make sense. Clarissa Pinkola Estés refers to the "unfounded fear" that many people feel about following their intuition, especially when it leads to unknown or uncomfortable choices.[46] But that fear is understandable. Listening to intuition is the easier part; the effort is in following up on its wisdom.

Often, the best thing we can do is maintain a stance on our intuition that is un-invested, and detached from the outcome. The minute we're too invested, we reduce the capacity to discern. Instead, we try to start from a default of curiosity or even trust (beginner's mind!). Discernment develops through the commitment to knowing oneself as authentically as possible and being willing to bear the risk of uncertainty, or of knowing something uncomfortable or challenging.

Trust is especially required when we are feeling uncertain, but the requirement for belief is minimized by focusing on lived experience. The proof is in the experience. Once we learn how to be in touch with inner experience, we can rely on that. This is not only empowering, it leads to a practical step in cultivating discernment: recognizing intuition when it happens.

As we have practiced in pillar 2, we need to let intuitive experiences happen; to experience our experiences. And as we explored in pillar 1, all of this is interfered with by beliefs about the trustworthiness of inner experience and stories we tell ourselves and others about 'reality,' especially when it comes to the non-ordinary realm of psychic experience.

One of the major obstacles to intuitive awareness is that we get in our own way with that all-too-familiar road blocker: doubt. Since intuition takes place on a level of awareness that exists largely outside of language, in the symbolic and energetic fields of experience, it can be tricky to not interfere by dismissing intuition too quickly. And in the other direction, it's important that we heed intuitive information. In extreme cases, not following our intuition can put us in danger, or even make us sick, when what we're refusing to let ourselves know settles into the body and becomes a tension pattern, inflammation, or irritation, a disturbance with potential to become disease.

But it's important to realize that discernment is different from doubt. If our goal is to enhance intuitive capabilities, we do not want to get caught up in *thinking* about intuition. We can get in our own way if we're too concerned with trying to understand what is happening when intuitive experience occurs. Instead, we need to welcome the non-rational, non-discursive experience as such, even if we don't quite understand what is going on.

Trusting our intuition involves accepting uncertainty and complexity as inherent features of reality. It helps to cultivate a willingness to consider things that might seem absurd or impossible at first. It also helps if we're willing to perceive the world as more profound than we often allow, more complex than we can even imagine, and more interconnected than we typically let ourselves perceive. If we expect this complexity and nonlinear unfolding, it is easier to trust. The mindset pillar helps us orient to this understanding; the discernment pillar helps us put this perspective into practice.

CONNECTING TO OUR INTUITIVE SELF

Trusting the experiences that make up intuition means we must be present to our lived experiences, even those we don't immediately understand (or those we don't like). If we have distanced ourselves from trusting our intuition, we will have constructed barriers to a range of other authentic human experiences as well.

In other words, disconnection from intuition is a symptom of wider disconnection from experience.

This disconnection is not a personal failing. It's baked into our culture, manifesting as anxiety and self-doubt. I often use the word 'alienation' to describe this experience, to suggest that our disconnection from intuitive experience is a result of internalized *cultural* factors—not a personal limitation. Alienation from intuition often takes the form of a fear that we can't tell the difference between intuition and anxiety or intuition and imagination. We worry that it's all in our heads. Is that creepy crawly feeling a weird manifestation of stress or is it a whisper that we should be paying more attention? Most of all, how do we tell the difference?

Psychic intuitive experiences are particularly troublesome. Are they real? Can you trust them? Are you a weirdo for having them? The answers to these anxieties lie in paying attention over time. First, we need to be aware of our inner responses to situations and remember that it's possible to connect what we feel in that moment to a manifest outcome. Specifically, we can learn to recognize our own intuitive tells.

From this point of view, cultivating discernment is like cultivating a relationship between parts of ourselves that may only usually communicate through dreams or visions—if at all. We can strengthen this relationship by accepting that non-discursive awareness exists and is real. We can send an internal memo that it is meaningful, even if the meaning is not translatable through words. This acceptance goes a long way towards inviting more of this type of experience.

So many of us do not feel confident in our ability to *hear* the inner voice, let alone trust what it has to say. We generally know there is a thing called intuition and that it is supposed to be valuable, but we are limited in how much we rely on it. We don't feel connected to it or recognize it as an important personal factor.

To be fair, there's a lot in the way:

- Our own biases, including a lifetime of belief and messaging about what consciousness can and cannot do.
- The habit of focusing our attention outside ourselves for knowledge and information—and the internalized assumption that that's where knowledge is found.
- Anxiety, fear, disengagement, and disconnection from our own inner experience.
- The habit of seeking comfort and simplicity rather than accepting complexity as a feature of lived experience.

DISCERNING VALIDITY THROUGH SELF-AWARENESS

The binary concept of right and wrong can be paralyzing. If I make a wrong choice, I have messed up, so I might not be willing to do the thing. I won't make that unconventional, surprising, inconvenient move because the risk is too great. But once we have integrated the concept of both/and nonduality, how might we then discern validity? This question becomes especially interesting when trying to discern pre-cognition or foreknowledge. How is it possible to trust that we know something that hasn't yet happened?

We can keep in mind that within the multiple planes of reality that exist simultaneously (such as in the implicate and explicate orders), something can be right and wrong at the same time. Something might be correct or true in the physical, immediate, explicate plane but not so in the cosmic, implicate order (Newtonian physics comes to mind). Discernment is supported by remembering that matter is more accurately understood as an event, or a field of energy, than a static 'thing.' So, whether we're talking about an object, an awareness, or information, it's more accurately a coherence of probability with expandable and permeable boundaries than 'real' in the concrete sense.

In many cases, rightness is context dependent. Something can be true for you and not universally true. Not everything that can be known is for everyone to know. We have to become more comfortable with this ambiguity as we transition from a binary-duality mindset to an inclusive, open, nondual one.

The question of how to know if an intuitive awareness is correct is sometimes a matter of personal ethics. Here, we encounter the deeply subjective nature of intuitive experience. For example, the 'truth' being revealed to you could be arising from your biases, the distortion your beliefs place on your perception, or a result of your unquestioned—or perhaps even false—assumptions. We believe a lot of things without realizing it, and these can add up to implicit bias, basically a distorted worldview built on inaccurate and unexamined assumptions.

The idea that knowledge should or can be neutral and that it somehow exists outside of (or despite) the people who use it is a fallacy. Intuition depends on the person (you, the subject) for its value. It does not work without us, since awareness is filtered through each person's lens and life. Intuition is influenced by personality, environment, and experience.

So the way subjective experience becomes trustworthy is through intentional self-awareness practice, where at the very least you become an expert of your own experience.

The difference between self-knowledge and self-awareness is relevant here. Self-knowledge implies that there is a self to know—in particular, a consistent, essential, kernel of individuality, usually understood to be comprised of ego, personality, and unconscious. This framing of self is misleading. For one thing, we are not individually constituted as 'selves' but are intricately interconnected—to our context and to (and through) other beings. For another, we are dynamic, changing beings, always in flux, so there is no permanent self-ness to know.

Self-awareness is more comfortable for me. It's more easily framed as a practice rather than as a destination or goal. Self-awareness, built on the assumption that the self is a dynamic construct, must be continually undertaken. It is a stance or process rather than an end point. Self-awareness includes awareness of the body, of thoughts, of relationships (ethics), of actions, of energy, of input, of output—all the processes that cumulatively comprise one's self.

Self-awareness is always ongoing work. Intuitive experiences can be difficult to trust, just as they can be difficult to perceive, because intuition is largely an unconscious process, and our self-awareness on that level tends to be extremely subtle and unpracticed.

As we change and develop, our perceptive awareness also changes, and we flow through times of more and less accessible intuition. We make intuitive decisions (or decisions we know are against our best interest), learn from them, and get feedback on and additional knowledge about our intuitive perception and how it works for each of us individually.

TRUST VERSUS DOUBT

Earlier, we looked at how an emphasis on doubt has seeped thoroughly into our culture. Collectively, we tend to value doubt over trust, and the habit of doubt has been internalized. Think about all the ways you don't trust yourself now. And all the ways you might not trust the world and its ability to support you. In some sense, a lot of this mistrust is absolutely justified. Living under a regime of colonial capitalism, we are profoundly disconnected from natural cycles, from our instincts, and from the impulses to nurture sustainable ways of living. And after a lifetime of experiencing disconnection from inner experience, it's understandable if you don't inherently trust your inner knowing.

As an academically trained philosopher and theorist, I have to admit that a part of me is reluctant to argue that truth is to be found in our subjective experience. This position can be weaponized as 'truthiness' or subjectivism, making it seem that objective reality is not real. But there is a difference between subjectivity and subjectivism. *Subjectivism* is where the concept of shared reality is totally dismissed. *Subjectivity* recognizes that we each read the world through our own unique experience. And subjectivity is necessary if we want to have a reliable connection to the intuitive aspects of our nature.

Am I suggesting that intuitive awareness doesn't conform to the same standards of knowledge we typically require for something to be true? Yes, yes I am. But I'm not trying to promote the idea that rationality and reason don't matter. Rationality and reason are wonderful, hard-won and evolved abilities, but they shouldn't simply replace inner knowing (also hard-won) because of a bias that it's a lesser form of knowing. Intuition and analysis are not binary; they're complementary and interconnected, supporting each other in a complex and holistic process, recursively informing each other. They are part of a skill set that makes good decisions, and that creates and comprehends knowledge.

One of the internalized habits of the scientific paradigm is the search for certain knowing. There is the idea that if something is true, it will always be true across any context, no matter who is perceiving, but this fallacy has been dismantled many times. For example, take the practice of medicine. We now know that women tend to experience symptoms and syndromes differently from men. This is true with heart attacks, diagnoses of neurodiversity, the experience of pain, and many other things. And that's just one possible category of difference.

Within an intellectual culture embedded in the dominance of analysis, intuition is often subjected to a special kind of heightened interrogation. How can it be true? How do you *know* it's true? These questions arise from assumptions about knowledge that are based in a positivist, materialist framework. But let's turn that around and view intuition through a transpersonal logic. The truth of intuitive experience relies on a coherent, contextual experience of the person who is intuiting. As opposed to materialist science that requires the subject be taken out of the equation, truth in this case necessarily depends on the subject. The context and the subject determine what is true and relies on a cared-for, self-aware, conscious person.

The thing about looking for truth in intuition is that its truth is founded on something other than objective measure. We can't go looking for the truth of intuition with the same standards of truth we use with objective, material matters. Scientist principles don't—and shouldn't—apply. Intuitive truth is subjective. It simply doesn't use the same rules as the reason or logic we are used to.

Uncertainty is a fact of our lives. The best theory we have confirms that, at least down at the quantum level, uncertainty is a fact. Becoming comfortable with uncertainty is an asset when you're working with intuition.

With intuitive experience, there's often an element of uncertainty involved. There's the complexity of needing to decipher the meaning of non-discursive content. There's the question of whether we trust ourselves enough to understand the intuitive experience on its own terms. Paradoxically, relinquishing the need for certainty and control creates the opportunity to experience more intuitive certainty, arising from a secure relationship between aspects of ourselves and a quality of trust in intuition.

Scientific inquiry typically involves intuition and its uncertainty at some point, whether in the initial creative stage of inventing experimental protocols to investigate a hypothesis or later, in working to interpret findings. Imagine a scientist following up a hunch to try a new procedure or to mix a certain chemical with another one. The alternative to experimental risks and guesses (or, as scientists like to call them, hypotheses) is getting mired by uncertainty and letting it cause anxiety. Clinging to security and safety would interfere with creativity and bring the development of new theories and ideas to an end.

Let's take an example of an intuitive hit. Imagine you're waiting for an elevator. It arrives, and just before you walk in, something in you registers the message, "Don't go in the elevator. Wait for the next one." Let's say you decide to listen to that inner knowing. You let the doors close and wait for the next elevator. Nothing out of the ordinary happens; the car you didn't get on doesn't come to an emergency stop. There isn't a $100 bill on the floor of the car you do get on. There's no discernible reason for the hit—so was it wrong? In a binary sense, maybe. There was no reasonable reason for you to take the next elevator. So how do you gauge the correctness of this hit?

First, let's remember the subjectivity of the experience. Notice that the hit didn't tell you about any danger. That's a layer of implication you might have drawn, based on your experience, your assumptions, your fears, etc.

Then, we can apply an intuitive logic. Within the old paradigm, we expect an intuitive hit to be right or wrong. Either there is a reason to not go in that elevator or there isn't. In the new paradigm, with the both/and logic of indeterminacy, it's impossible to say that your intuition was incorrect since we can never know what didn't happen. There's no way of knowing whether there was a reason to steer clear of that first elevator car. We have to choose to trust that it's valuable to listen—even if we never know why.

Advocating for trusting intuition is not the same as suggesting that we completely give up the analytic way of knowing nor the cognitive approach to perception. Not at all. I'm not advocating for scientists to quit measuring and triangulating their results and instead follow their hearts. Nor do I think any of us should quit thinking for the sake of intuition-driven living. Our ancestors worked hard to develop the analytic abilities we rely on, and they're our birthright!

But I *am* advocating for being more intuitive. This is not either you're intuitive or you're analytic. We are all capable of being both, and we need to accept this.

Analysis is also always an imperfect translation. It is never a capture of the thing itself, but it is always in some way mediated, whether through judgment, assessment, reason, or thinking (all secondary processes that take place after intuition or sensation provides the input[47]).

Here's an example of using intuition versus a rational mode to make a decision. Let's say I want to decide where to go on vacation. I can gather a list of features about each of these places and evaluate which one checks the most 'dream vacation' boxes. I can make a list of pros and cons to sort out all the reasons each location is a good choice. I can consult with friends, do research, or call a travel agent to get input about the best deals. (These would be the analytic approaches.)

Or…I can consult with my body, checking in about how each of the options feels to my sensorium and nervous system. I can use any number of divination tools—dowsing, tarot, scrying—to invite the unconscious to participate in the decision-making process using its communicative methods. (These intuitive approaches rely on senses, colours, shapes, feelings, and vibe rather than language or metrics.)

Both decision-making processes can work. Either is a valid approach to decision-making. But used in collaboration, they can become even more reliable. Intuitive and rational modes can act as checks for each other. One choice might look good on paper but cause a constrictive feeling in the belly, a clear tell that the intuitive mode is communicating its dissent in its non-rational way.[i]

---

[i] This is apparently Warren Buffett's tell when he makes decisions about the stock market and his investment strategy.

INTERPRETING AND ACTING ON INTUITION

There's a moment in the intuitive process where we have to allow the experience to happen without trying to analyze or comprehend it. It's important to avoid the urge to represent the experience to ourselves prematurely. When experimenting with our own intuitive abilities, we can become better at simply paying attention and noticing the experience, before evaluating, judging, attaching language, applying concepts, or assigning a category to the experience. In this way, a focus on the experience itself can lead to immediate, direct perception of the world we are attending to.

But then, we have to not only let ourselves feel those (admittedly sometimes weak) signals, we also have to recognize them as intuitive, and then feel authorized and liberated enough to take that awareness seriously.

There comes the time to make sense of the experience, a process of discernment that improves with intentional practice of self-development and self-awareness—paying attention to who you are, how you show up, what you do, the tender and tricky aspects of yourself, your blind spots, your habits, your fears.

The reason we develop a practice of self-awareness is so that we can decipher what the unconscious communicates and what it means…to us. We might be used to thinking about the unconscious as inherently pathological or suspicious. But the unconscious is not necessarily what's repressed, it's merely what is unknown—or yet unknown. The psyche is a storehouse of fears, shadow elements, perversions, desire, and collective pain. It's also rich in symbolic meaning, archetypes, depths, and wisdom.

Psychologists and philosophers in the transpersonal tradition, like Stanislav Grof and Abraham Maslow, have urged us to "de-pathologize" the psyche, to frame it as a source of health and creativity rather than of darkness or illness. Grof reframes the experience of hearing "too much" from the psyche as "spiritual emergency" rather than as psychological breakdown. Often, psychological dis-ease is the result of not being adjusted to aspects of society; there's nothing inherently wrong, just a mismatch. Ideally, such maladjustment alerts the rest of us to problems with society itself and the ways we are collectively organizing ourselves and relating to each other and the larger world. It's not that there is a problem with the individual person; there's a problem with the way we've structured our communities and societies.

The purpose of an examined life, the foundation of psychological maturity, is to engage in the process of working to make the unconscious conscious. And for me, this points directly to the self-awareness work of discernment. Cultivating intuitive awareness is inherently tied to this process of development, as the emergence of mature self-authority lets us trust in our own psyche.

The transpersonal worldview is helpful here. Attending to what *is* through non-judgmental awareness primes our attention to notice what's happening. This practice might help us learn what a feeling feels like—in the body, in the psyche, or both. This is not only about intuition but about how we inhabit ourselves in our everyday lives. For example, many of us hold stress in the body; the shoulders, neck, and jaw are notorious for this. Oftentimes, simply noticing this tension starts the process of releasing it. But now we recognize that the body holds information. All experience is stored in the body, including the stuff that happened to our ancestors! It might become possible to identify if the stress isn't our own, but something picked up from the collective. Or it might be ours but from a long time ago, the result of a stressful experience now passed. We might be experiencing something today that simply needs to be expressed so that it can move on, move through.

With attention and self-awareness, we can learn to discern what needs to be worked on and what needs to be worked out. This means figuring out our feelings and following them, rather than what many of us do: run away from them. It means engaging in self-inquiry to find out more, and staying curious about our experience, even when (especially when) it is difficult or challenging.

PRACTICES FOR DISCERNMENT

Various forms of creative expression help us engage with the non-discursive, nonlinear, intuitive parts of our selves. These practices support discernment, as they help us decipher the symbolic structures through which we make meaning. When we draw, write, dance, or dream with the intent of cultivating intuition, we are communicating to the intuitive self that we are making an effort to learn its language. This effort gets rewarded with more fluency in the non-discursive realms.

Other forms of helpful practice include anything that leads to greater self-awareness. Contemplative and reflective inner work show us the patterns of our thoughts. We learn what we think, desire, and fear, and learn to recognize the stories we tell about our experience. We weed and cultivate the garden of the mind, as they say.

Within the intuitive mode, something can be true or real symbolically or mythologically without being specifically, literally accurate. This again points to the need for a process that encourages us to trust non-discursive content as meaningful. It also calls for the need to feel our feelings, and especially, to know ourselves. The discernment pillar invites us into exploration, experimentation, and, often, moving slightly out of our comfort zones.

Three themes characterize the practices for discernment:

Mindfulness, paying attention within. For developing self-awareness and for getting better at recognizing our tells, feelings, thoughts, proclivities, etc. We've already talked about how meditation works to cultivate the witness consciousness. Journaling is another form of self-reflection that can help you to learn about your own mind.

Experimenting, or 'researching.' To learn our own, unique intuitive style. Acting on intuitive hits and observing what happens. You might keep an intuition journal, recording successes and failures. Make the intuitive body into an ally in consciousness. Be curious about what yes and no feel like. Practice recognizing what resonance feels like.

Creative expression. Communicating and interpreting our non-discursive experience. Speaking or writing about what your intuition reveals, or using poetry or painting or some other art form. You might look for a listening partner, someone trustworthy who also values these kinds of experiences. Together, you might find yourselves creating language for what you mean in new and interesting ways, even if you previously thought the experience was not languagable.

KEEPING AN INTUITION JOURNAL

As you take on this praxis of connecting more deeply with your intuitive nature, take notes. Keep a record of what you notice, what you make of it, and the outcomes of any actions you take as a result.

By paying attention to what happens, we can create a record of evidence to review as we work to make sense of the experience.

A lot of the time, people don't realize they've had an intuitive hit until later. Only then can they point to the experience and say, "Oooooohhhhh. So that's what that was." To cultivate intuition, it's helpful to track the sense of intuition as it arises. I describe this as building a bridge to that experience. If you can map what it felt like (in retrospect), you are better able to recognize it in real time the next time.

We keep an intuition journal to record intuitive awarenesses so we can look them up later and even confirm whether they were accurate. The journal becomes a track record of successes, failures, missteps, and nuance. It becomes a bridge to our previous insights and helps us connect intuitive experience and our subsequent actions—and it helps us figure out and reflect on whether something was 'right' to act on. Keeping a record this way lets us look back and see the process of our development.

And over time, we build our own vocabulary and narrative of intuitive experience: *This is what it felt like just before this happened. This is when I realized it, but I didn't admit it to myself until later.* And so on.

This practice works on a second level because of the recursive feedback loop of attention. By keeping a journal, we maintain the intention to record intuitive hits. Because we know we're going to be recording any and all intuitive experiences, we become more alert to intuitive experiences as they happen, and will likely notice more of them.

FREE WRITING

Free writing is a way of journaling with the intent of letting the subconscious speak. We put the pen to the page and let it fly. When free writing, try to write without stopping until a self-imposed limit (whether a certain number of minutes, or filling a certain number of pages).

Free writing helps cultivate heightened awareness of inner states, assumptions, and experiences. Over time, this technique helps us develop the habit of thoughtful insight and allows us to interpret intuitive content more responsively and responsibly. It also becomes a form of paying attention because the practice leads us to become increasingly self-aware.

To access intuitive awareness from deep within, let your subconscious know that you are interested and are open to its awareness. Free writing is a way to engage with ourselves that gives our intuition permission to express itself openly. Whatever arises is welcome. We put aside the critical part of our minds—at least temporarily. (This part of us is often satisfied to wait, knowing that it is just resting and can come out later.)

Free writing helps us connect with the non-linguistic, non-discursive aspects of intuitive knowing. It lets us become more familiar with how we make sense of symbolic structures, both collective and personal, and tends to dig out our (frequently unconscious) assumptions, beliefs, desires, and habits.

LEARN WHAT INTUITION FEELS LIKE FOR YOU

Thinking back to the phenomenology of intuition, do you know what it feels like to be in an intuitive moment? How do you know when a fuzzy, subtle, or non-discursive awareness is intuition? How do you know if it is simply a shiver, a muscle contraction, or gas?

There's no limit to the embodied and psychic cues that might be available to trigger us into paying attention, that signal an intuitive experience is happening, that tug on our sleeve and point us to intuition-in-action. There are likely as many unique tells as there are humans. Gut feelings, butterflies, tingles, goosebumps, or whatever might signify something specific, or they are simply alerting us that there is something to know here, something to pay attention to. The important thing is to learn what your own characteristic tells feel (smell, look, sound) like and then decide to trust them as valid and valuable information.

Most people have at least one intuitive experience they can point to as an example of what I'm talking about. Sometimes, these are experiences of an inner voice that guides us to do (or not do) something. Sometimes, we feel the intuitive sense like a compass or a magnet, showing us the way.

For example, one day I was looking for my partner's keys. *Something* told me to check under a sweater on the chair, even though he had already looked there. I was drawn in that direction, and when I lifted the sweater, there they were. The intuitive self knew and drew me towards my target.

Many intuitive experiences are way less specific. It's possible to register a hit and know there is something to know…without knowing what it is we're supposed to know. This is where practice becomes incredibly useful. First, we need the ability to recognize an embodied signal. This itself is an experience. Then, we need the ability to recognize that the signal is significant, or meaningful, beyond just a sensation.

EXPERIMENT AND PLAY

Becoming more receptive to intuitive experience is supported by experiment and play. Games can also help us practice discernment. Guessing games are an excellent way to train this muscle. They exercise that part of us that *can* know, but while the stakes are low; they are just games. For example, with TV shows, try to guess what is going to happen next. When your phone dings, guess who's reaching out before looking at the display. Guess which elevator is going to come first. Which grocery line will move the fastest. Etc. Games like these help us become familiar with what it feels like before we are right, and what it feels like to have certainty in our knowing, compared with the natural feeling of a mere guess.

As with learning any new way of being, attitude is important. An attitude of open curiosity is most helpful. Getting frustrated or impatient or expecting too much? Not helpful. Be gentle, yet persistent—just like when you're learning any new skill. The attitude of play or lightheartedness helps because it can be very difficult to discern your intuition when you're emotionally invested in the situation.

Sometimes people are good at staying out of the way of their intuition, refusing to let their mind interfere with creative response. I'm thinking of things like how, in extreme situations, intuition can guide a person to step out of the way of an impending crash or to leave home at just the right moment so they bump into a long-lost friend on the corner (an example of synchronicity, an instance of unconscious intuitive action). Those involved in improvisational arts know exactly what I mean here: Intuitive movements can occur at any time, to anyone.

And speaking of improvisational arts, we can use them to cultivate discernment by practicing our faculty with both/and, nondual logic. We can experiment with saying "yes, and" (the improv rule!) and find ways to enlarge our perspective on whatever is presenting.

LETTING A PROBLEM SIMMER

Incubation is the practice where, after a period of working on a problem, we let it go. We do something else and let the intuitive self get to work. Adopting a receptive attitude intentionally and taking the directed mind out of the equation yields interesting and surprising results.

There's a story about August Kekulé[48], the organic chemist who discovered the molecular structure for benzene. Famously, the benzene ring structure is said to have been revealed to Kekulé in a daydream reverie. The insight arrived in the form of an image: the ouroboros, a snake eating its own tail. Kekulé allowed this insight to inspire his thoughts about the problem, not in a literal, signifying way but in a symbolic, imaginative way. And it led him to his discovery. Here we can see the structure of discernment at work: he needed to first accept the image as potentially meaningful and then figure out how it connected to the situation at hand.

Kekulé's moment of insight didn't come out of the blue; he had already been working on the problem and had set it aside for the time being. This example of incubation highlights the need for rest and for leisure. Taking a break is a well-known strategy among artists and high-level executives alike. Discernment—interpretive insight—requires space and time. For our intuition to be in good shape, the mind needs downtime to float or wander.

Chapter 8
INTUITION ON ITS OWN TERMS

The emergent intuitive paradigm has become much more prevalent in recent years. More and more, people seem on board with the framework that lets intuition make sense, and are waking up to their intuitive potential. It's exciting. New paradigms, perspectives, and possibilities that were previously unthinkable and unimaginable are opening up, and reminding us that we are intuitive.

Since 2022, I have been teaching the three pillars for cultivating intuition in a group coaching program. The program was designed to address the biggest problems most people have with becoming more connected to their intuition:

- Internalized beliefs and habits related to not trusting ourselves as knowers;
- Not being familiar with the range of unique and subjective ways we can experience intuition; and
- Not realizing that intuition is a relationship we can cultivate through inner work.

All kinds of people benefit from intuition development practice: people who are intuitive (and even psychic) but who need validation to own the authority of their inner knowing; and people who don't realize they're intuitive, who benefit from an initiation into that relationship.

It seems strange that we would need to cultivate intuition on purpose, but we do. Without our intuitive function active and online, it can be hard to know what's best for us. It can be hard to make decisions. We run our brains around in circles trying to make up our minds. We've been in a dysfunctional relationship to the intuitive function for a long time now. We value it but don't know how to relate to it. And while we assume we should just know what it is—and even shame ourselves for neglecting intuitive messages—we also crave trusting it more.

We need to do this intentional work of cultivating intuition in order to unlearn internalized scientism and to disentangle ourselves from the hyper-rationality of our culture. This is a worldview that shapes us and our ways of being, even structuring what we dream of, what we desire, and what we think of as possible.

We end up taking for granted things like the idea that time works in a one-dimensional, linear direction, or that space is composed of three dimensions (even when physicists tell us there are many more dimensions than this and that a more accurate picture of reality reflects a non-linear, nondual, quantum flow). And even though we live in and within this flow, we tend to habitually perceive, believe, and think that the world exists in discreet and discontinuous parts.

We think of ourselves this way, too. Although human beings are interdependent and relational, we habitually think of ourselves as individuals and strive for independence or pursue 'self' development as if that's a possibility separate from interconnection with the collective. Believing this about ourselves, we minimize the resonance and connection available to us (not to mention that the presumption of separateness can throw us into chaos when we find ourselves in uncertain situations because it leaves us without a sense of anchor in the world).

So yes, we need to do the work of cultivating intuition.

When I teach this work, I typically start by having participants share their intuition stories. Even people who think they're not intuitive usually have some story to tell. Sometimes, hearing someone else's story sparks a memory or a realization: "Oh, that was intuition!?" We tell our stories to normalize them. We realize how common they are. We also share our intuition failures—times when we "should" have listened but didn't—so we normalize that, too. There's healing in sharing stories of our inner process.

I ask participants (and I'm asking you) to consider their lived experiences of intuition (their intuition stories) as primary pointing devices. To cultivate intuition, we start with the experience and then make sense of it, unfolding a recursive relationship over time with that part of you that just knows. That's why this book starts with what intuitive experience is *like*. The common gestures that make up intuitive experience—being in a flow state, being holistic in all senses of that word, creative awareness, meaning-making, receptivity to vibes—none of these are material. They're not easily visible, and we have to intentionally learn to identify the experience, so we know what to look for when it shows up.

Until we connect to intuition on its own terms, mainstream and mass market concepts and ideas about intuition will continue to alienate us from intuitive experience, based in the conflict between how we expect intuition and how we experience it. We either learn that intuition is unreal and too 'out there' or else it's not flashy enough to be noticed. Starting with the experience also helps us overcome the taboo around the 'woo' of intuition.

I call the first pillar of practice, mindset, because it's about how we think about intuition—what it is, how it works—but it also concerns our attitude and beliefs about it. If we're talking about vibes, resonance, and energy, are you willing to engage with those ideas as valid and legitimate? Or do you resist the woo factor? Do you own up to what you believe about the multiverse and your experience in it? These questions help us develop a framework that embraces intuition as complex and holistic. An intuitive mindset doesn't reduce the world to binaries but lets it be complex and alive with creative potential. This is the quantum-akashic framework—or, simply, intuition on its own terms.

Intuition on its own terms points us to the infinite nuance that exists in the world, nuance that our minds might someday be capable of knowing…if we allow that truth exists along a spectrum of potential, always incorporating a degree of uncertainty, and appearing to each of us through our unique, culturally informed perspectives. I've suggested an akashic metaphor because it allows for what is yet-unknown to also exist. It points to how foreknowledge and other prescient forms of intuition are possible—via energies that haven't yet emerged from domains of potential. Akashic awareness presents the self as capable of intuition because it is an integrated, interconnected whole.

In considering what intuition is, I've asked you to look at your beliefs and metaphysical choices and to consider incorporating ideas that might seem strange (or maybe even wild) at first, because intuition *is* metaphysical (or transpersonal). Intuition shows us our connection to other dimensions of experience, layers of consciousness beyond the physical: whether that's to a part of our own mind-heart-body-being; consciousness shared among individuals or groups of people; or that which arises from perceiving collective currents, shared conscious content, or patterns of coherence. The good news is, ironically, we can overcome our fear of the weirdness by embracing the non-ordinary, parapsychology of it all; if we allow ourselves to accept that consciousness is much more interesting and wacky than we typically give it credit for.

Once we accept a theory of intuition on its own terms, we're primed for the ways we can experience intuitive content and the intuitive mode. What seems to be required for intuitive development is shifting the way we relate to ourselves as knowing subjects. We need to see ourselves as having agency, power, and the self-authority to trust our knowing.

When we acknowledge intuition on its own terms, we see that, more than anything else, intuition is a way of being. Rather than a source of information per se, or a skill or ability, intuition is a part of our nature as embodied, conscious beings. The practices we engage with to become more intuitive—inner work, mind-body stuff, breathwork, energy practice—all of these make us more coherent so we can resonate as and with the information that vibrates through and around us.

It's a flow we can get into.

In any intuition workshop, we always spend some time learning how to focus and calm our minds. We prepare ourselves to experience extended consciousness, using meditation or other contemplative practices that help us become aware of our inner process.

Maybe the most difficult part of the work (and why it's not achieved in a single workshop but over time, through mentorship and ongoing reflective practice) is practicing self-awareness, becoming more thoughtful experts of our own minds and interpretive lenses. Self-awareness is the basis of the discernment pillar, where we cultivate a relationship of trust with ourselves so we can more skilfully accept what we have come to know intuitively.

In the workshop, I pose the question of how we know intuition is trustworthy. Trusting ourselves becomes a way of healing from the mythos that we are separate and that we don't matter. With intuition on its own terms, I've presented a way of understanding how to establish and assess that trust. We have to consider whether the person doing the intuiting is trustworthy, how big of a lens we are using to assess, and whether we are willing to trust what is unseen, among other things. Getting better at knowing the difference is a matter of diligent, intentional practice in self-awareness and in tracking the outcomes of intuition over time.

Participants reflect on times in their lives when they haven't listened to their inner knowing and times when they have. They journal, pay attention to their inner experience, and connect with the feelings that have alerted them to their intuition in the past. Usually, they realize how some of their beliefs about intuition have interfered with knowing themselves as intuitive. Through this reflective inner work, we make ourselves conscious of our own connection to the intuitive mode.

The work of cultivating intuition on its own terms is both political and spiritual. But this is an existential spirituality we're talking about: Secular, scientific, and pluralist, this is the sense of connection and meaning woven throughout mystical traditions and philosophies.

I think of intuition as spiritual in part because of the element of trust involved in perceiving things in the unseen, symbolic realm. Trust in this case is akin to belief. There's always a period of uncertainty once you've experienced the intuitive insight but before its content is confirmed as accurate.

Spirituality is also embedded in the holistic nature of intuitive experience, where we feel that information arrives through the body, mind, or spirit (often all at once). This can be a source of confusion because not all intuitive insight is spiritual. (As a mode of connection between the self and a greater awareness, the intuitive *mode* is spiritual, but the content need not be.)

The politics of intuition are maybe less obvious.

Can you imagine a world where people recognize the complexity and unseen elements of our world? Or a world in which people trust their inner knowing, feel connected to an existential sense of spirituality, and include their dreams, visions, and insight as motivation for choices in their lives?[i]

If we accepted our interconnectedness as a fact, how might we act? How would we conceive of ourselves? What extended states or stages of consciousness might become available?

Our allegiance to objective knowledge production has taken us collectively to the brink of literal disaster and, in some cases, right through to disaster-level circumstances. Climate chaos, inequality and injustice, and violent conflicts all arise from justifying actions with rational analysis. The consequences of internalized rationality are not only personal. They're political.

As we deepen our connection to intuition, we deepen our relationship to life itself. Becoming more intuitive and trusting our intuitive nature will effectively open the world to us, reveal more of what there is to know, and facilitate a more expanded,

---

[i] If questions like these are as exciting to you as they are to me, the readers' discussion guide (available at www.WhatIsIntuition.ca) is a great resource to inspire conversation and inquiry around these themes.

expansive imagination so that we inhabit the world in wonder and deep connection. This could even generate an overall shift in consciousness.

In our world right now, there's a need to find balance between analytic and intuitive ways of knowing. We need to give ourselves permission to know what we know, yet not let every thought, feeling, or impulse go unexamined. An intuitive approach to knowing responds to that balance by emphasizing a relational process rather than an outcome. It's a path that rests on developing a self-aware agency that centres the self and our experiences and allows us to trust our experiences, even when they don't make ordinary sense.

Because here's the thing. When we internalize that everything is connected and shares in some aspect of consciousness (though not necessarily self-conscious awareness), there's a vast potential for fellow feeling. The assumption of human-centredness is diminished. And that's a realization that can offer a profound existential context; we literally cannot live without each other and all the other life of this world. We are all part of a fractal, holographic universe, rich with unseen energies. And while most of us usually do not perceive the energies, symbols, and vibrations that make up the nonlinear flow of experience, it doesn't mean we aren't moved by them. Nor does it mean we're unaware of the information they convey.

Intuition is a relationship we have with ourselves. It's a mode of connection, an experience reliant on resonance throughout the 'vibro-sphere' of the unseen dimensions, both within and beyond space-time.

The trick is making space for it in our lives and in our culture. That's when we can experience the full spectrum of consciousness in which intuition thrives—and makes sense. On its own terms.

GLOSSARY

Alienation: Disconnected. An existential condition related to disenchantment, an outcome of living within a mechanistic world view and the belief that it's possible to know everything that exists. Connected to a cultural critique about the conditions of our lives. How we live, as if we are disconnected, and how that effects what we do. The feeling that our lives don't matter. Often produces anxiety and loneliness.

Dimension: A distributed domain or extent of vibrating coherence. A field is flat but a dimension spreads out in all directions. When I refer to the seen (versus the unseen) dimensions, I mean the material world that we tend to think about as 'real'—things we can touch, smell, taste, hear, etc., and that other people can also touch, smell, taste, hear. The unseen dimension is also known as the implicate order (Bohm, 1980), a domain of infinite potential.

Epistemology: A branch of philosophy concerned with theories of knowledge. It asks what distinguishes true knowledge, belief, and opinion, and considers the origins and limits of what we know.

Hegemony: Prominent or dominant. Refers to the way cultural dominance is achieved through popular uptake of an idea, value, or rule. The way I'm using it is to refer to a dominant ideology or accepted norm; something that is so widely accepted it seems inevitable or invisible to the casual observer.

Intra-action: I use this word after Karen Barad, a philosopher whose theories of knowing and being rely on quantum principles. The prefix intra- means from within (whereas inter—refers to between), so the word intra-action suggests that each agent effects the other, and both (or all) are changed in the process. Intra-action recognizes the nondual inseparability (the entanglement) of the subject & object, and that the relationship of the actors is what makes the intra-action possible.

Metaphysics: A branch of philosophy concerned with the ultimate or fundamental nature of reality. Here, metaphysics describes the characteristic of being more-than-physical, a coherence that is greater than but also encompassing the physical, material dimension.

Non-discursive: A quality or state of being for which we don't have much language. Often refers to states of mind achieved through meditation or other non-ordinary states (dreams, trips, dissociations). Experiences that don't lend themselves to language, concepts, structures, or stories. Subtle, indistinct, or happening in a dimension of experience that doesn't 'do' words.

Phenomenology: A branch of philosophy concerned with the study of phenomena as we experience them, and the meanings things have in our experience. As a methodology, it aims to study subjective experiences (consciousness, perception, emotions, etc.) as objectively as possible.

Praxis: Engagement or action done with the intent to enact change in the world. Putting ideas or theories into practice, or deliberately living out one's values in the world. For Paulo Freire, praxis meant a recursive, reflective practice where theory and action inform each other.

Psyche: Greek for 'soul.' Colloquially, we use the word to refer to 'mind,' as in psychology. But more accurately, according to C.G. Jung, psyche is a holistic conglomerate of body-mind-soul and includes both conscious and unconscious content.

Scientism: Excessive or dogmatic belief in the power of science and scientific methods. The idea that all knowledge production must conform to scientific knowledge and techniques in order to be valid.

Self: An individual person, often defined in contrast to 'other.' However, an akashic framework reveals that self and other are convenient distinctions rather than metaphysical truths. When the word appears with a capital S ('Self'), that usually refers to the whole or 'higher' self, in recognition of the self being connected to the more-than-self dimensions, i.e., a transpersonal self. Generally, self is our personality, beliefs, values, actions, and relations. The Self is the entirety of our makeup.

Spirituality: Spirituality is an awareness of, and the pursuit of, meaning. Here, I'm talking about a secular spirituality, so the sense of meaning is not necessarily one of divinely ordained purpose or order but rather a sense of coherence or complexity that each of us participates in by virtue of our consciousness.

Spirituality is the lived experience of being aware of this connected context. It is an awareness or recognition that even though we usually identify as our individual self, there is a greater, underlying (or over-lying) part of that self that is, at the same time, an interconnected part of everything else.

Intuition is spiritual in the transpersonal or metaphysical sense: It's an experience of knowing that arises from being connected to something *more*.

Tell: In stage magic, a tell is a subtle gesture that discloses (usually not on purpose) how the trick is done. Here, it's a signal or sign that alerts us to intuitive experience. Common intuitive tells are gut feelings, flushes, tingles, or changes in the breath. There are probably as many unique tells as there are people, even though a tell is not always present in many intuitive experiences.

Transpersonal: States of consciousness (and their contents) beyond personal identity. The prefix *trans-* means beyond. So transpersonal means beyond the personal. But it shouldn't be understood as hierarchically above and beyond. Trans- here means transcends and also includes. For example, the unseen dimensions transcend but also include space-time.

A lot of transpersonal stuff is collective human stuff that connects us to each other, beyond time and space. Elemental stuff, the energies of things, personal history, collective history, archetypes, myths, spirits of all kinds, etc.

Woo (or woo-woo): A synonym for spiritual, mystical or metaphysical. Often deployed as a casual insult.

Worldview: The entirety of our beliefs about what the world is and how it works. Embedded in stories, language, religion, and values. Sometimes explained as the water we swim in, because we don't know it exists until we encounter a different one.

I first learned this word in an introductory Indigenous studies class, and it gave language for something I learned the first time I tried psychedelic mushrooms: that the reality we know about is conditioned by what we believe about the world, including our own individual nature, human nature, and nature in general. It's possible to become aware of our own worldviews, but we have to know to look for them.

ENDNOTES

1. Rich, A. (1979). Women and Honor: Some Notes on Lying. in *On Lies, Secrets & Silence: Selected Prose*. pp 185-194. New York: Norton & Co.

2. Bai, H, Scott, C. & Donald, B. (2009) Contemplative Pedagogy and Revitalization of Teacher Education. *The Alberta Journal of Educational Research*, 55 (3), 319-334.

3. Ahenakew, C., de Oliveira Andreotti, V., Cooper, G. & Hireme, H. (2014). Beyond Epistemic Provincialism. *AlterNative*, 10(3), 216-231.

4. Bastick, T. (1982). *Intuition: How we think and Act*. Toronto: John Wiley & Sons.

5. Jung, C.G. (1971). *Psychological Types*. (R.F.C. Hull, Trans.). Princeton, NJ: Princeton University Press. (Original work published 1921).

6. Estés, C. P. (1992). *Women who Run with the Wolves: Myths and Stories of the Wild Woman Archetype*. New York, NY: Ballantine.

7. Petitmengon-Peugot, C. (1999). The Intuitive Experience. In F. J. Varela and J.Shear (Eds.), *The View From Within: First-person approaches to the study of consciousness* (pp. 43-77). Thorverton, UK: Imprint Academic.

8. Sheridan, J. & A. Pineault. (1997). Sacred Land – Sacred Stories. In R. David-Floyd and P.S. Arvidson (Eds), *Intuition: the inside story*. (57-80). New York, NY: Routledge.

9. Laszlo, E. & Dennis, K.L. (2013). *Dawn of the Akashic Age: New consciousness, quantum resonance, and the future of the world*. United States: Inner Traditions.

10. Goswami, A. (2017). *The Everything Answer Book: How quantum science explains love, death and the meaning of life*. United Kingdom: Hampton Roads.

11. Laszlo, E. (2014). *The Self-Actualizing Cosmos: The Akasha revolution in science and human consciousness*. United States: Inner Traditions.

12. Bradley, R.T. (2007). The psychophysiology of intuition: A quantum-holographic theory of nonlocal communication. *World Futures*. 63(2): 61-97.

13. Laszlo, E. & Dennis, K.L. (2013). *Dawn of the Akashic Age: New consciousness, quantum resonance, and the future of the world*. Inner Traditions.

14 Goswami, A. (2017). *The Everything Answer Book: How quantum science explains love, death and the meaning of life.* Hampton Roads

15 Sheldrake, R. (2003). *The Sense of Being Stared At.* London, UK: Random House.

16 Kishkinev, D. et al. (2021) Navigation by extrapolation of geomagnetic cues in a migratory songbird. *Current Biology. 31(7): 1563-1569.*

17 McCraty, R. (2015). *Science of the Heart, Volume 2.* https://www.heartmath.org/research/science-of-the-heart/energetic-communication/

18 Bradley, R.T. (2007). The psychophysiology of intuition: A quantum-holographic theory of nonlocal communication. *World Futures.* 63(2): 61-97.

19 McCraty, R. (2015). *Science of the Heart, Volume 2.* https://www.heartmath.org/research/science-of-the-heart/energetic-communication/

20 Guertz, K. (2002). Culture and the Senses: Bodily Ways of Knowing in an African Community. Berkeley, CA: UC Press.

21 Chalmers, D. (2007). The Hard Problem of Consciousness. In M. Velmans and S. Schneider, (eds.), *The Blackwell Companion to Consciousness. (pp.* 225-235.). United Kingdom: Blackwell.

22 Hunt, T. and J. Schooler. (2019). The Easy Part of the Hard Problem. *Frontiers in Human Neuroscience.* Volume 13 - 2019 | https://doi.org/10.3389/fnhum.2019.00378.

23 Hunt, T. (2018). The Hippies Were Right: It's All About Vibrations, Man. *Scientific American.* https://blogs.scientificamerican.com/observations/the-hippies-were-right-its-all-about-vibrations-man/

24 Ibid.

25 Bohm, D. (1980). *Wholeness and the Implicate Order.* London, UK: ARK.

26 Bradley, R.T. (2007). The psychophysiology of intuition: A quantum-holographic theory of nonlocal communication. *World Futures.* 63(2): 61-97.

27 Goswami, A. (2017). *The Everything Answer Book: How quantum science explains love, death and the meaning of life.* United States: Hampton Roads.

28 Laszlo, E. (2014). *The Self-Actualizing Cosmos: The Akasha revolution in science and human consciousness.* United States: Inner Traditions.

29 Goswami, A. (2017). *The Everything Answer Book: How quantum science explains love, death and the meaning of life.* United Kingdom: Hampton Roads.

30 Buhner, S.H. (2004). *The Secret Teachings of Plants.* Rochester, VT: Bear & Company.

31 Ibid.

32 Laszlo, E. (2014). *The Self-Actualizing Cosmos: The Akasha revolution in science and human consciousness.* United States: Inner Traditions.

33 Sheldrake, R. (2012). *The Science Delusion: Freeing the Spirit of Enquiry.* United Kingdom: Coronet.

34 Laszlo, E. (2014). *The Self-Actualizing Cosmos: The Akasha revolution in science and human consciousness.* Inner Traditions.

35 Ferguson, M. (1987). *The Aquarian Conspiracy.* Los Angeles, CA: J.P. Tarcher.

36 Freire, P. (1970/2011). *Pedagogy of the Oppressed.* New York, NY: Continuum.

37 Ahenakew, C., de Oliveira Andreotti, V., Cooper, G. & Hireme, H. (2014). Beyond Epistemic Provincialism. *AlterNative*, 10(3), 216-231.

38 Targ, R. (2012). *The Reality of ESP: A Physicist's Proof of Psychic Abilities.* Wheaton, IL: Quest.

39 Kincheloe, J. L. (2010). *Knowledge and Critical Pedagogy: An Introduction.* New York, NY: Springer.

40 Buhner, S.H. (2004). *The Secret Teachings of Plants.* Rochester, VT: Bear & Company.

41 Ibid.

42 Kincheloe, J. L. (2010). *Knowledge and Critical Pedagogy: An Introduction.* New York, NY: Springer.

43 Csikszentmihalyi, M. (1990). *Flow: The Psychology of Optimal Experience.* New York, NY: HarperCollins.

44 Sheldrake, R. (2003). *The Sense of Being Stared At.* London, UK: Random House.

45 Watts, A (1966). *The Book: On the Taboo Against Knowing Who You Are*. UK: Jonathan Cape.

46 Estés, C. P. (1992). *Women who Run with the Wolves: Myths and Stories of the Wild Woman Archetype*. New York, NY: Ballantine.

47 Jung, C.G. (1971). *Psychological Types*. (R.F.C. Hull, Trans.). Princeton, NJ: Princeton University Press. (Original work published 1921).

48 Goldberg, P. (1983). *The Intuitive Edge*. Los Angeles, CA: J.P. Tarcher.

SELECTED BIBLIOGRAPHY

Ahenakew, C., de Oliveira Andreotti, V., Cooper, G. & Hireme, H. (2014). Beyond Epistemic Provincialism. *AlterNative*, 10(3), 216-231.

Anderson, R. & W. Braud (Eds). (2011). *Transforming Self and Others Through Research*. Albany, NY: State University of New York Press.

Bai, H, Scott, C. & Donald, B. (2009) Contemplative Pedagogy and Revitalization of Teacher Education. *The Alberta Journal of Educational Research*, 55 (3), 319-334.

Barad, K. (2007). *Meeting the Universe Halfway: Quantum Physics and the Entanglement of Matter and Meaning*. Durham: Duke University Press.

Bastick, T. (1982). *Intuition: How we think and Act*. Toronto: John Wiley & Sons.

Bauman, Z. (2007). *Liquid Times*. Cambridge, UK: Polity.

Bergson, H. (2007). *An Introduction to Metaphysics*. (T.E. Hulme, trans.). J. Mullarkey and M. Kolkman, eds. London, UK: Palgrave Macmillan.

Bohm, D. (1980). *Wholeness and the Implicate Order*. London, UK: ARK.

Boucouvalas, M. (1997). Intuition: The Concept and the Experience. In R. David-Floyd and P.S. Arvidson (Eds), *Intuition: the inside story*. New York, NY: Routledge.

Bradley, R.T. (2007). The psychophysiology of intuition: A quantum-holographic theory of nonlocal communication. *World Futures*. 63(2): 61-97.

Buhner, S.H. (2004). *The Secret Teachings of Plants*. Rochester, VT: Bear & Company.

Choquette, S. (2004). *Trust Your Vibes: Secret Tools for Six-Sensory Living*. Carlsbad, CA: Hay House.

Csikszentmihalyi, M. (1990). *Flow: The Psychology of Optimal Experience.* New York, NY: HarperCollins.

Day, L. (1996). *Practical Intuition.* New York, NY: Villard.

Dweck, C. (2007) *Mindset: The New Psychology of Success.* New York, NY: Ballantine.

Ferguson, M. *(1987). The Aquarian Conspiracy: Personal and Social Transformation in Our Time.* Los Angeles, CA: J.P. Tarcher.

Freire, P. (2011). *Pedagogy of the Oppressed*, 30th Anniversary Edition. M. Bergman Ramos, (Trans.). New York, NY: Continuum.

Gawain, S. (2000). *Developing Intuition: Practical Guidance for Daily Life.* Novato, CA: New World Library.

Gee, J. (1999). *Intuition: Awakening Your Inner Guide.* Boston, MA: Weiser Books.

Geurts, K. (2002). *Culture and the Senses: Bodily Ways of Knowing in an African Community.* Berkeley, CA: UC Press.

Goldberg, P. (1987). *The Intuitive Edge.* Los Angeles, CA: J.P. Tarcher.

Goswami, A. (2017). *The Everything Answer Book: How quantum science explains love, death and the meaning of life.* Hampton Roads.

Greene, M. (1995). *Releasing the Imagination.* San Francisco, CA: Jossey-Bass.

Grof, S. (1993). *The Holotropic Mind.* With H. Zina Bennett. New York, NY: HarperCollins.

Grof, S. (1998). *The Cosmic Game.* Albany, NY: SUNY Press.

Grof, S. (2008) 'Birthing the Transpersonal.' In *The Journal of Transpersonal Psychology*, Vol. 40, No. 2 155-177.

Joye, S.R. (2020). *The Electromagnetic Brain: EM field theories on the nature of consciousness.* Inner Traditions.

Jung, C.G. (1971). *Psychological Types*. (R.F.C. Hull, Trans.). Princeton, NJ: Princeton University Press. (Original work published 1921).

Kincheloe, J. L. (2010). *Knowledge and Critical Pedagogy: An Introduction*. New York, NY: Springer.

Laszlo, E. (2014). *The Self-Actualizing Cosmos: The Akasha revolution in science and human consciousness*. Inner Traditions.

Laszlo, E. & Dennis, K.L. (2013). *Dawn of the Akashic Age: New consciousness, quantum resonance, and the future of the world*. Inner Traditions.

Mariechild, D. (1981). *Mother wit: A Feminist Guide to Psychic Development*. Trumansburg, NY: The Crossing Press.

Miller, J. P. (1994). *The Contemplative Practitioner*. Toronto, ON: OISE Press.

Naparstek, B. (1997). *Your Sixth Sense: Unlocking the Power of Your Intuition*. San Francisco, CA: Harper.

Orloff, J. (1996). *Second Sight*. New York, NY: Warner Books.

Palmer, P.J. (1993). *To Know as We Are Known*. New York, NY: HarperCollins.

Palmer, W. (1994). *The Intuitive Body: Aikido as a Clairsentient Practice*. Berkeley, CA: North Atlantic Books.

Peirce, P. (1997). *The Intuitive Way*. Hillsboro, OR: Beyond Worlds.

Petitmengin-Peugot, C. (1999). The Intuitive Experience. In F.J. Varela and J. Shear (Eds), *The View From Within: First-person approaches to the study of consciousness* (pp. 43-77). Thorverton, UK: Imprint Academic.

Pinkola Estés, C. (1992). *Women who Run with the Wolves: Myths and Stories of the Wild Woman Archetype*. New York, NY: Ballantine.

Pollen, M. (2018). *How to Change Your Mind: The New Science of Psychedelics.* London, UK: Penguin.

Rich, A. (1979). Women and Honor: Some Notes on Lying. In *On Lies, Secrets & Silence: Selected Prose.* Pp. 185-194. New York: Norton & Co.

Salk, J. (1983). *Anatomy of Reality: Merging of Intuition and Reason.* New York: Columbia University Press.

Schulz, M. (1998). *Awakening Intuition.* New York: Three Rivers Press.

Sheldrake, R. (2003). *The Sense of Being Stared At.* London, UK: Random House.

Sheldrake, R. (2012). *The Science Delusion.* London, UK: Hodden & Stoughton.

Sheridan, J. and A. Pineault. (1997). Sacred Land – Sacred Stories: The Territorial Dimensions of Intuition. In R. David-Floyd and P.S. Arvidson (Eds.), *Intuition: the inside story.* (pp. 57-80). New York, NY: Routledge.

Starhawk. (1988). *Dreaming the Dark: Magic, Sex and Politics.* Boston, MA: Beacon Press.

Suzuki, S. (1970). *Zen Mind, Beginner's Mind.* New York, NY: Weatherhill.

Tart, C.T. (1992). The Physical Universe, The Spiritual Universe, and the Paranormal. In C.T. Tart (Ed.), *Transpersonal Psychologies.* (pp. 113-152). New York, NY: HarperCollins.

Vaughan, Frances E. (1979). *Awakening Intuition.* New York: Anchor Books.

ACKNOWLEDGEMENTS

Writing this book has been a labour of love, and I'd do it again in a minute.

I want to honour the dear colleagues who supported and inspired me as I initially worked through these ideas in the academy and beyond. Deep gratitude to my clients and students with whom I've been refining and testing these ideas over the years, and who have taught me so much about what intuition looks and feels like in real life.

The entity that is One Can Press managed to gather an incredible coven of a production team. Thank you to my editors: Tracie Kendziora, creative genius who also wrote the readers' guide (download it from my website!) and Eleonore Presler. (the Clarity Maven), brilliant philosopher who generously walked with me through a painful and necessary re-structuring early on. Thank you to the beta readers, whose fresh eyes helped me write in a kinder (or sometimes, less kind) voice. Thank you to the design team at fleck creative and Umbrella Squared Design Group, who nailed the vision. Thank you to Jennie Alexis, who helped me get the book into your hands, in as graceful a way as possible.

Love and so much appreciation to my family and friends, who endured years of the messy process while loving me anyway. And especially to Martin, for incomparable care and for holding the vision and the spirit of this project this whole time; I wouldn't have done this without you.

Dedicated to the return of the Great Mother, and to an intuitive way of being in the world.

EMILY SADOWSKI, PHD (she/they) writes, teaches, and mentors smart, sensitive leaders in cultivating self-awareness and self-compassion so they can connect with—and trust—their inner knowing. Obsessed with leadership and the transformative inner work that leads people and cultures to change, Dr. Sadowski's work sits at the intersection of spirituality, meaning-making, existentialism, and collective liberation. Connect with her at www.emilysadowski.com.

www.ingramcontent.com/pod-product-compliance
Lightning Source LLC
Chambersburg PA
CBHW031107080526
44587CB00011B/863